Modern Design

R. CRAIG

PHOTOGRAPHS BY

MODERN

IN THE METROPOLITAN

The Metropolitan Museum of Art, New York

MILLER

Mark Darley

DESIGN

MUSEUM OF ART 1890-1990

Harry N. Abrams, Inc., Publishers, New York

IN MEMORIAM

Frances V. Middleton Calhoun
1921–1972

PUBLISHED BY
The Metropolitan Museum of Art, New York
John P. O'Neill, Editor in Chief
Barbara Burn, Project Coordinator and Editor
Nai Chang, Designer
Helga Lose, Production

Published in 1990 by The Metropolitan Museum of Art and by
Harry N. Abrams, Incorporated, New York, a Times Mirror Company

Library of Congress Cataloging in Publication Data

Miller, R. Craig.
    Modern Design in the Metropolitan Museum of Art (1890–1990)
/ R. Craig Miller; foreword by Philippe de Montebello; photographs by Mark Darley.
       p.   cm.
    Includes index.
    ISBN 0-87099-598-7. — ISBN 0-87099-599-5 (pbk.). — ISBN
0-8109-3612-7 (Abrams)
    1. Design — History — 20th century. 2. Metropolitan Museum
of Art (New York, N.Y.)   I. Metropolitan Museum of Art
(New York, N.Y.)
    II. Title.
NK1390.M54 — 1990
745'.09'040747471 — dc20   90-6293
                                        CIP

The color photographs in this book were taken by Mark Darley; the
black-and-white photographs were taken by The Photograph Studio,
The Metropolitan Museum of Art.

Front endpaper: Anonymous Russian: Textile, ca. 1900. Gift of
Monique W. Wiedel, 1980 (1980.267)

Back endpaper: Robert Venturi, American: "Tapestry" Textile, 1984.
Gift of Knoll International, 1987 (1987.383)

Binding stamp based on Edgar Brandt, French: "Perse" Door, ca. 1923.
Edward C. Moore, Jr., Gift, 1924 (24.133)

Caption type set by Meriden-Stinehour Press, Lunenburg, Vt.
Text set by U.S. Lithograph, typographers, New York, N.Y.
Color separations by Reprocolor International, s.r.l., Milan, Italy
Printed and bound by Amilcare Pizzi, S.p.a., Milan, Italy

Contents

Foreword

With the opening in 1987 of the Lila Acheson Wallace Wing, the Metropolitan Museum at long last had a permanent gallery in which to display its Modern design and architecture collection. This space has made it possible for objects that had not been on view for several decades to be shown on a rotating basis, although they can impart only a hint of the remarkably rich collection that the Museum has amassed over the last century.

It gives me great pleasure therefore to introduce a book that presents an extraordinary number of masterpieces from the collection that we would never have the space or ability to display simultaneously. Although not a catalogue raisonné, this book does reveal the vast range and depth of material that the Museum has acquired, most of it in the design and architecture collection of the Department of Twentieth Century Art but a great deal of it also drawn from other parts of the Museum — the American Wing, the Costume Institute, the Department of European Sculpture and Decorative Arts, and the Department of Prints and Photographs.

The history of the Museum's commitment to Modern design, as outlined in Craig Miller's essay — indeed, the fact that it was a major area of interest — will come, I expect, as a surprise to many. Even before the turn of the century, the Museum had begun to acquire fine objects soon after they were made, a tradition that continues today. Of greater importance were a series of annual exhibitions of industrial design that ran from 1917 to World War II and the beginnings, in 1922, of a comprehensive Modern design collection. It was only in 1967, however, that the Museum finally created a department devoted exclusively to twentieth-century art.

During the last decade, the Museum's activity in the field of Modern design has reached a new intensity, especially in the acquisition of works representing the whole range of styles and modes that have developed over the past century. Not surprisingly, many of the objects illustrated in this book have been acquired since 1983, clearly reflecting the interests of the author, who has been a driving force behind the Museum's effort to form an extensive collection of twentieth-century design.

I would like to take this opportunity to express on behalf of the Museum our deep gratitude to a number of individuals who have played a crucial role in assembling this collection. Major funds have been established in the name of Edward C. Moore, Jr., Edgar Kaufmann, jr., Edward Pearce Casey, Theodore R. Gamble, Jr., the Hazen/Polsky family, and the Irving Wolf family, and these have enabled the Museum's curators to acquire an impressive range of works. Important international donors to the Twentieth Century Department in recent years have included Mr. and Mrs. Melvin Bedrick, Michael Chow, Ernesto Gismondi, Michael Heller, Mr. and Mrs. Douglas Heller, Jack Lenor Larsen, Mr.

and Mrs. Cleto Munari, Mr. and Mrs. Peter Palumbo, Addie Powell, Nan Swid, Mr. and Mrs. Robert Venturi, and Paul F. Walter. A number of donors have given objects to the Museum specifically for this book and deserve special thanks: Emilio Ambasz, Casas-Barcelona, Mr. and Mrs. Monte Factor, Grand Cypress Hotel Corporation, Dr. and Mrs. Charles Hardy, Mrs. Larry Horner, James R. Houghton, Emily Fisher Landau, Martinelli Luce, Claes Oldenburg, Lisa Licitra Ponti, Simon International, and Coosje van Bruggen. The Metropolitan Museum is greatly indebted to these patrons.

Now, with the publication of this handsome book, the reader may study and enjoy what the visitor would not be able to view on one or even several trips to the Museum itself.

PHILIPPE DE MONTEBELLO
Director

Perceptions of Design

More than two centuries ago Western society underwent fundamental changes with the advent of democratic governments, the Industrial Revolution, international economies, and a large, educated middle class. In terms of the arts, these forces soon necessitated a reordering of the relationship between the applied arts and other art forms — painting, sculpture, and especially architecture. Decorative designers and craftsmen had long worked in a collaborative but largely secondary position with other artists. The emergence of the architect as designer, as well as of the industrial designer, profoundly altered the status of everyday objects. Moreover, mass production, new materials, and international marketing now made it possible for well-designed furniture, ceramics, textiles, and even glass to be accessible to the masses. Thus by the mid-nineteenth century, design had become one of the first truly democratic art forms and would be followed in subsequent decades by posters, photography, and film. In the United States, The Metropolitan Museum of Art was among the earliest art institutions to grasp this fundamental shift in our culture brought on by the Modern Movement. This book examines the evolution of our concept of design over the last one hundred years and documents the role that the Museum has played in this process — both active and inert at different times. This catalogue is, therefore, not a history of Modern design but rather an introduction to a complex discipline using the Metropolitan's history and collections as a fulcrum.

William S. Lieberman, Chairman of the Department of Twentieth Century Art, is responsible for initially suggesting this project. He had originally envisioned an issue of the Museum's quarterly *Bulletin* that would record the history and diversity of the Metropolitan's Modern design collections, but over the last two years the idea grew into a more ambitious catalogue that would explore these two issues in greater detail. The first section of the book concisely documents the Museum's involvement in Modern design from the late nineteenth century to the present, in terms of its collections, exhibitions, educational programs, and philosophical approaches. The second part is presented as a pictorial survey of selected masterworks, since the diversity of the holdings is perhaps best understood visually. To furnish a structural framework for this pictorial survey, the hundred years under consideration have been broken into three chronological divisions, with the world wars as breaking points. Each of these periods was further divided into stylistic sections to reflect many of the major aesthetic movements that occurred concurrently.

The first two sections in each division generally treat fully developed styles, major movements with serious intellectual and philosophical underpinnings, which for the most part span all the arts, including architecture and urban planning. The other sections in each of the chronological periods suggest less recognized modes, or manners, which are usually more ephemeral and limited in scope. While often decorative in nature, these modes may nonetheless have had a significant influence in the applied arts. Although the Museum's collection consists of a wide variety of works, only ten categories of objects are represented in each section: glass, ceramics, metalwork, lighting, textiles, costume, architectural drawings, decorative drawings, furniture for sitting, and other furniture forms. These categories nonetheless provide a broad survey of the applied arts field.

The choice of a single object for each category was a difficult and, in some cases, arbitrary decision. The Museum's collection in many areas has extraordinary depth, and numerous masterworks could have been chosen for most categories. The primary objective of this book, though, was to illustrate the broad range of the Metropolitan's holdings, not to provide a catalogue raisonné. Final choices were also dictated by a number of other factors: a desire to show the international scope of a particular style or mode, a wish to include many of the major designers of the Modern Movement, and a need to reevaluate artists who have been neglected. It should be noted that some artists have occasionally been placed in sections where they are perhaps not most often associated. Again, the goal has been to represent larger design movements, not to provide surveys of individual artists' careers.

Photography of the objects was a central task in the production of this book. It was decided to commission all new color photographs, including numerous details and alternate views. These pictures were not to be typical record shots against gray, seamless paper but were intended to be expressive of the object and its period. Many pieces were photographed with other objects in the collection. The creation of this visual section of the book was therefore an unusually complex task, where the design of the photographs and the book itself were approached with considerable care.

A few words about terminology and the formation of the collection are also in order. The Metropolitan has over the decades used the terms "applied arts," "decorative arts," "industrial arts," and "design" virtually synonymously. The name "applied arts" is perhaps the more inclusive and most telling, since it makes clear the fundamental distinction from the fine arts with its implication of function. Yet the Department of Twentieth Century Art has elected to use the term "design" for its holdings. The collection, in fact, consists of three distinct divisions. Decorative design is defined as objects conceived by one person but made by another; these are generally handmade in limited production, and such luxury items constitute a large segment of the collection. Industrial design likewise consists of objects conceived by one person but made by another, but these products are intended for mass production. Both divisions imply an intellectual process whereby ideas are transferred by a series of drawings to the fabricator. Craft, on the other hand, constitutes a third division, where the objects are conceived and made by the same person, often simultaneously and as one-of-a-kind pieces.

The department has in recent years consciously chosen to broaden its parameters to form a comprehensive collection, one that would be inclusive of the variety of design approaches and stylistic movements that have evolved in this century. Modern design has not been a monolithic or linear development, and at least four major issues have confronted artists in cyclical swings through the decades: the fascination with new technology and mass production, the study and adaptation of historical styles, the concern for the relationship of humanity to nature, and the ephemeral but often influential crossover from painting and sculpture to the applied arts. The Metropolitan's holdings seek to reflect this constant flux: within any given style, the sole criterion for inclusion in the collection is one of quality.

Judging an object thus becomes the crucial question for any curator. Art museums are fundamentally different from science and history museums in their emphasis on aesthetics. To form a coherent collection, curators need parameters to judge innumerable pieces from different cultures, and in recent years the department has developed a checklist for analyzing objects under consideration. While there are two-dimensional design objects, most applied arts are three-dimensional and may be viewed in terms of the following criteria:

FORM

COMPOSITION

How does a piece rest on a surface, unfold into a three-dimensional body, and finally resolve itself at its apex?

MODELING

Is the treatment of mass linear, planar, or plastic? Is there an overall sense of massiveness or delicacy? What is the play between positive mass and negative space?

INTEGRATION

What is the degree of articulation between major and secondary elements in the composition? How are parts joined together?

PROPORTION

What is the fractional relationship between parts? Are elements exaggerated, truncated, etc.?

SURFACE

MATERIALS

What substances have been chosen and how have they been juxtaposed? Is an object opaque, translucent, or transparent?

PATTERN AND ORNAMENT

Is an object embellished with two- or three-dimensional decoration?

COLOR

Is an object monochromatic or polychromatic? Are the colors primary or muted?

TEXTURE

Is an object smooth or rough? Has one substance been employed or a multiple of materials with differing textures?

FINISH

In terms of reflectiveness, is an object matte or polished?

CONSTRUCTION

CRAFTSMANSHIP

What is the overall quality of the execution? Was the object designed to be made by hand, machine, or a combination of the two?

BASIC BODY

How has the underlying structure been made to receive the finished surface?

EXPRESSIVE USE OF MATERIALS

Have the innate qualities of the substance been exploited — whether they are wood, plastic, metal, glass, clay, or fiber? How have the materials been cut, bent, extruded, cast, laminated, woven, or blown?

TECHNOLOGY

Has a material been exploited in a new manner to create a design object? Has the innovative use of a material allowed the creation of a new form?

UTILITY

FUNCTION

Is the object conceived of as utilitarian or ornamental? If the former, what is the degree of comfort and usefulness?

ECONOMY

What is the relationship between price, quantity of material, time expenditure, and the number of objects produced?

MAINTENANCE

What degree of care is required to maintain an object in good condition? What longevity is envisioned for the piece: i.e., was it conceived of as disposable or lasting?

CONCEPT

PRECEDENT

Does the designer rely on historical sources or consciously seek to create something new?

ICONOGRAPHY

Was there a conscious choice of imagery which has religious, political, etc., overtones?

APPROACH

Has the designer approached the creation of the object from a moralistic or formalistic perspective? Does the piece have economic, ergonomic, and political overtones or was it conceived purely in visual terms? Could the object have been conceived from a "non-design" reference point, like a sculpture or painting?

Lastly, a few general remarks should be made about the position of design in American museums. Only a few institutions in the United States are devoted exclusively to the applied arts, and, within most art museums, the decorative arts have long been subordinated to the fine arts in regard to gallery space, exhibition slots, and funding. In terms of twentieth-century design per se, the situation is especially unresolved. There are surprisingly only a handful of American museums — unlike our European counterparts — that have even begun to think seriously about the formation of comprehensive applied arts collections, when the last one hundred years have constituted one of the greatest periods of accomplishment in the history of Western design. This predicament is particularly incongruous when we consider how many museums — even regional institutions — have large departments devoted to twentieth-century painting and sculpture.

A number of factors have led to this situation, one of the most obvious being museum organization. Following the model of the Victoria and Albert Museum in London, a number of design collections are divided into separate departments by medium, such as textiles and architecture. Such divisions make it difficult to form comprehensive collections, particularly when numerous artists have worked in more than one medium. Also, many departments are set up by nationality, which works against the formation of international collections. Some museums have likewise elected to collect or exhibit only one aspect of design, whether it is a single material, style, or time period. At the Metropolitan Museum itself, the Modern collection is divided among five curatorial departments: American Decorative Arts, European Sculpture and Decorative Arts, Costume Institute, Prints and Photographs, and Twentieth Century Art. This setup was an arrangement that simply evolved, rather than being deliberately thought through. A coherent, organized structure is, in short, critical for the formation of a well-rounded collection of twentieth-century design.

There are also a number of issues outside the walls of museums that must be identified if Modern design is to ever be accepted by our cultural institutions as a major force in this country. These issues reflect a lack of awareness — if not resistance — in our very society. For example, the American government — unlike those in Europe and Japan — does not really consider the design industry to be part of our national identity or even an important factor in our economy; one has only to think of French couture, Italian and Japanese industrial design, or the national design councils in Scandinavia and Britain.

Within the art market itself the applied arts are considered less valuable than the fine arts. A design object may be purchased for only a fraction of the cost of a painting, drawing, or sculpture by artists of comparable merit. Because monetary values are indicative of what a capitalist society considers important, the message is transmitted to museums in a multitude of overt and indirect ways. Moreover, it is difficult — if not impossible — to study the applied arts at the graduate level within art-history departments at many of our major universities; many of these same departments have large faculties to teach twentieth-century architecture, painting, sculpture, and photography. Even architectural history is most often taught as a study of facades or plans; interiors and furnishings are rarely treated, although many architects have designed their buildings as total ensembles. Such value judgments shape our culture and are not easily changed.

Given this perplexing situation, it is thus all the more remarkable that the Metropolitan has amassed such a refined and wide-ranging twentieth-century design collection. The early trustees and staff conceived of the Museum as a positive force in American society, as a reformer and tastemaker — an educator in the truest sense. Design was perceived then as the most democratic of all the arts, for it was readily accessible to almost every citizen. In succeeding decades, this concept would fall into disfavor at the Museum, and the mantle would be taken up by other American museums. By the mid-1960s, however, the Metropolitan rediscovered its activist past, and design returned as a subject of serious debate at the Museum, one that has continued to the present. Perhaps no other art form is so clearly subject to the forces of lifestyle, aesthetics, economics, and technology yet so concisely reflects the changing perceptions of our culture.

The Metropolitan Museum of Art in 1880, designed by Calvert Vaux and Jacob Wrey Mould

Modern Design at
The Metropolitan Museum of Art

For the generations born after World War II, the Metropolitan Museum's name is hardly synonymous with Modern design, yet from its founding in 1870 this institution was one of the first major museums in America to make a commitment to the field of contemporary applied art. In the last 120 years, the Metropolitan has amassed a modern collection of several thousand objects and has mounted some 125 exhibitions (see Appendix A) devoted to or including design after 1890. The strength of this commitment to Modern design has, however, been inconsistent over the decades, as the concept of the Museum's mission in our society has evolved. This essay chronicles the remarkable story of the individuals and ideas that have defined this long-neglected chapter in the Metropolitan Museum's history.

1870–1905

The idea of an art museum for New York City was first suggested in Paris on July 4, 1866, by a prominent lawyer named John Jay, and four years later The Metropolitan Museum of Art was incorporated. The first Board of Trustees was made up largely of major civic leaders, but it also included five noted American artists: Frederic Church, John Kensett, John Quincy Adams Ward, Frederick Law Olmsted, and Richard Morris Hunt. The Charter was short but emphatic in setting forth the Museum's mission:

> The Metropolitan Museum of Art [is] to be located in the City of New York, for the purpose of establishing and maintaining in said city a Museum and library of art, of encouraging and developing the study of the fine arts, and the application of arts to manufacture and practical life, of advancing the general knowledge of kindred subjects, and, to that end, of furnishing popular instruction and recreation.[1]

In the Annual Report of 1872, the Trustees went further in describing their hopes for the new museum.

> The Trustees of the Museum purpose to establish an institution which, at some distant day shall combine the functions of the British National Gallery and the Art Departments of the British Museum and the South Kensington Museum [now the Victoria and Albert Museum]. They desire, in the first place, to collect and publicly exhibit adequate examples of the ancient and modern schools of painting and sculpture, and, secondly, to provide as large and complete a collection as possible of

objects which, without coming within the class just mentioned, derive their chief value from the application of fine art to their production — in short, a representative Museum of Fine Art applied to Industry.[2]

From the beginning, therefore, the Trustees envisioned an art museum in which fine and applied arts would be given equal importance. This commitment to "the application of arts to manufacture and practical life" was typical of late-nineteenth-century museums in America. Their models were the Victoria and Albert Museum in London (founded 1852) and its European offshoots — the Union Centrale des Arts Décoratifs/Musée des Arts Décoratifs in Paris (founded 1864) and the Österreichisches Museum für Angewandte Kunst in Vienna (founded 1864). Although modest in terms of building and funding, these Victorian art museums were almost messianic in their desire to reform society. Such institutions were often founded in cooperation with their governments in order to encourage national industries associated with the applied arts. The museums maintained schools for teaching artists and craftsmen, and they attempted to raise the level of public taste among artisans and manufacturers, as well as consumers. In startling contrast to present-day practices in art museums, collections and exhibitions were assembled as much for didactic as for aesthetic purposes.

Given these precedents, it is not surprising then that one of the first actions taken by the Metropolitan's Trustees — anticipating their move in 1880 to a new building in Central Park designed by Calvert Vaux and Jacob Wrey Mould — was the establishment of a school for the industrial arts and the acquisition and exhibition of an industrial arts collection.[3] Also, from the 1870s onward, the Museum began sporadically to acquire examples of contemporary design in various styles and media. These early acquisitions were not the result of a master plan so much as happenstance, but they formed an important basis for a Modern design collection that was catholic in scope.

In April 1879 the Trustees defined their ideas for an industrial arts collection. To establish a collection exhibiting the progress and position of the Industrial Arts. To include in compact form in each department, the raw material, the material in process of manufacture, and the completed work, with models or samples of the tools and machinery used. This collection to comprise, among other articles, Gems, Gold and Silver Work, Bronzes and other Metal-Work, Household Decorations, such as Paper Hangings, Pressed Leather, Furniture, etc., Textile Fabrics, Bookbinding, Laces, Dyes, Stained Glass, etc.[4]

Professor Thomas Egleston of the School of Mines at Columbia University was asked to gather objects for this collection. The first installation was less than hoped for, but at least the Museum had made an initial commitment to forming an instructive collection.[5] It is interesting to note that the Egleston selection gave equal emphasis to the process of manufacture and to the finished product. Today it is only the latter that falls within the usual purview of an art museum.

Plans for an industrial arts school were discussed by the Trustees in 1879 and a modest enterprise, funded by a grant from Gideon F. T. Reed, was begun the following year in facilities outside the main building. The school would last fourteen years. The first classes were free and included sessions in woodwork and metalwork. In 1881 the curriculum was expanded to include: "Drawing and Design; Modeling and Carving; Carriage Drafting; Decoration in Distemper; and Plumbing."[6] Artist and artisan alike were thus welcome at the Metropolitan.

The Museum administration recognized early on that American designers and manufacturers relied heavily on foreign industries. The Trustees noted in 1881 that "the time has certainly arrived when America should cease to be dependent upon foreign production of beautiful works in any and every department of industry. . . . If American industrial art is to rank with that of European countries, it can only be by having educated artisans."[7] Implicit in these early statements by the Trustees are two important concepts that would become policy during the first half of the twentieth century: the Metropolitan Museum as educator of the American public and as a major force in shaping American society.

By 1887 the Industrial Art-Schools had grown considerably in size and scope. A faculty of thirteen now offered a variety of courses for students ranging from beginners to public-school teachers. The curriculum included classes in "Color; Design; Modeling; Free-hand, Architectural, Cabinet, and Mechanical Drawing; Chased and Hammered Metals; Carved Work-Tiles, Textiles, etc."[8]

Two years later the school was moved into the Museum building, where students would have immediate access to the collection for study. The latter point became a critical issue in the 1890s for the Trustees, who saw the curriculum moving away from its relationship to the Museum collections.[9] By 1894 the decision was made to close the Industrial Art-Schools, but not without some reservations. In the next Annual Report, the Trustees called for a School of Architecture to be affiliated with the Museum.

> Permanent quarters with a proper organization for employing teachers and giving elementary instruction should be provided in a building near enough to the Museum to secure the advantage of our casts and models, library and apparatus. This splendid opportunity for usefulness is recommended to individual or corporate effort; and the Trustees would welcome an alliance which would make the suggestion effective.[10]

Apparently this call went unheeded, and an important chapter in the Museum's history was closed within a quarter of a century, as the Metropolitan began to modify its commitment to the applied arts.

One permanent record of those formative years is the initial acquisitions, which were largely American and remarkably eclectic.[11] These objects now form the core of the late-nineteenth and early-twentieth-century collection in the Department of American Decorative Arts. Two early gifts of special note are a telegraph originally thought to have been the first instrument by Samuel F. B. Morse (figure 1) and material given in honor of Cyrus W. Field to commemorate the laying of the Atlantic cable. These were perhaps the Metropolitan's first examples of product design. In the 1870s and 1880s, the Museum received a number of gifts that are paradigms of late Victorian taste, among them a pair of chairs made for the Centennial Exposition in Philadelphia by Pottier and Stymus (figure 2).

These acquisitions are indicative of an important aspect of the Museum's collecting policy: its ready acceptance of, if not preference for, decorative and historicizing design.

1. Telegraph, 1837–44, attributed to Samuel F. B. Morse. Gift of George Hutchins, 1876 (76.7)

3. Vase, ca. 1896, by Louis Comfort Tiffany. Gift of H. O. Havemeyer, 1896 (96.17.10)

2. Armchair, ca. 1875, by Pottier and Stymus. Gift of Auguste Pottier, 1888 (88.10.3)

The Metropolitan was by no means opposed to more innovative design, however, and in the following decade it acquired a number of examples of Art Nouveau, including a series of favrile glass pieces made by Louis Comfort Tiffany for H. O. Havemeyer (figure 3). With the start of a new century, the Metropolitan Museum was to enter another phase, one in which it grew from being merely a national museum to an institution of international importance.

1905–1917

J. Pierpont Morgan was elected President of the Metropolitan Museum in 1904 and Robert W. de Forest was named Secretary. Morgan held office until his death in 1913, but de Forest's service to the Museum would last for another thirty years. He succeeded Morgan and became one of the most forceful presidents in the Museum's history. During the first decades of the new century the Metropolitan became an immensely wealthy institution through a series of bequests, each in the millions of dollars.[12] This funding enabled the Museum to undertake an ambitious acquisitions program, a major building expansion, and the establishment of a first-rate professional staff.

In 1905 the Museum named the English architect Caspar Purdon Clarke as its new Director. The choice of a designer to run the Metropolitan was a clear sign of the Trustees' intentions. In the Annual Report of 1905 it was noted:

> The election as our Director of Sir Caspar Purdon Clarke, lately head of the South Kensington Museum, in the collections of which "Industrial Art" takes so important a place, should be a sufficient guarantee that these branches also will have due consideration. They are generally subordinated to the other better known and more popular lines of museum development because, though frequently no less esthetic, they are as frequently utilitarian. They should, therefore, have for our own practical countrymen not only the attraction of beauty but the added interest of close relation to our industrial development as a nation.[13]

Other notable appointments quickly followed: Edward Robinson, director of the Museum of Fine Arts in Boston, was named the Assistant Director and head of the Department of Classical Art in 1905; Roger Fry, the noted British art critic, was placed in charge of the Paintings Department in 1906; and Wilhelm R. Valentiner, who had trained at a number of German museums, was named the head of a new Department of Decorative Arts in 1907.[14] Two years later Joseph Breck, who was soon destined to play a major role at the Museum, was hired as Assistant Curator of Decorative Arts.[15]

At this time the Museum made two important contemporary French acquisitions. The first was a Sèvres vase of 1904 by Fernand Thesmar (figure 4); the second was a stained-glass triptych, *La Danse des Fiançailles*, of 1885 by Luc Oliver Merson (figure 5). Both pieces illustrate the conservative taste of the Museum during this period.

Perhaps the most significant appointment of the decade was the hiring of Henry W. Kent in 1905 as Assistant Secretary. Kent would shape policy at the Museum for thirty-five years. Along with Alfred H. Barr, Jr., the founding director of the Museum of Modern Art, Kent forged an active mandate for American museums in Modern design for the first half of the twentieth century.[16] In an institution as large as the Metropolitan, many individuals have been involved in determining policy, but Kent's leadership was

4. Vase, 1904, by Fernand Thesmar.
Gift of Mrs. Charles Inman Barnard,
in memory of her mother-in-law,
Susan Livingston Barnard, 1905 (05.10.1)

5. "La Danse des Fiançailles" Triptych, 1885, by Luc Oliver
Merson. Bequest of Adelaide Mott Bell, 1906 (06.292a–c)

among the most discernible in word and deed. Two of his basic principles deserve to be examined here, since they relate so closely to the applied arts.

First, Kent perceived that American art museums were fundamentally different from their European counterparts in terms of their mission for society. He was opposed to a museum where "art [was] for art's sake," rather than "art for the people's sake."[17] Kent wrote in his autobiography:

> It was plain to see that a public institution of art was, in the last analysis, a public servant, and that the things to do were the things which worked for the public welfare. The old idea of the museum as a storehouse of art laid it open to the criticism that it would become a mausoleum in fact unless it was made to be actively serviceable. In other words, the European idea of a museum of art which housed the treasures the country had accumulated by hook or by crook, museums like the Vatican and the Louvre, did not fit the needs of this country, which had its own arts to develop. The American museum should show collections of what other civilizations had done, under religious or civil influences, of course, as a lesson to those whose business it was to produce similar kinds of things for us, to show what had been done and what might be done, by our own artists and craftsmen. Thus the museum would become a teacher in the truest sense, which was a new idea in this country — the active teacher instead of the inactive opportunity.[18]

Kent went on to quote an article of 1936 in which he felt the author summarized his approach succinctly:

> Mr. Kent divides museum functions into three parts. The first is acquisition. When the Met builds an American Wing and stocks it . . . that is acquisition. The second is exhibition, which is putting things out where people can see them conveniently and to good advantage. This is old stuff. . . . But the third function is exposition — trying to get people to see what the exhibits mean, giving them a chance to use them, apply them in their businesses or professions, work them into their daily lives. That is new.[19]

To accomplish his goals Kent created a professional administrative structure for the Metropolitan, a system that has now become so familiar in other museums in this country that it is taken for granted, as if it had always existed. To make the Museum accessible and usable, Kent set up a card-catalogue system for objects, standard printed labels for objects on exhibition, an information and sales desk, and an editorial department and Museum press, as well as a publications program. This book is, in fact, printed in the Centaur typeface, which Kent encouraged Bruce Rogers to design and which he purchased for the Museum's exclusive use in 1914. Within a decade Henry Kent had executed profound changes in organization:

> The Museum was coming out of its brick-and-stone shell. It was putting its collections to work. It was making people see what the past has to do with the present: not the past of books, which are sometimes hard to read, but the past of the things books tell about, with the brush marks, scars of the chisel, toolings, weavings and embroideries of patient, long-vanished fingers still visible.[20]

Nowhere was this development more evident than in the field of applied arts; for Kent, "the museum's place [was] in the active, working, producing world of design today,"[21] and he embarked on an ambitious program that would utilize the full scope of the Museum's potential. Three years after the Department of Decorative Arts was opened in 1907, it moved into a new wing. In 1905 Kent opened an educational division in order to reach out to schools and the general public, for which he served as Supervisor of Museum Instruction from 1907 to 1925. About 1904 the Photograph Studio was organized, followed by a Lantern Slide Lending Collection two years later, making images of objects in the collection readily available for study. A new library wing was opened in 1910, greatly expanding that essential resource for students and designers. Six years later a Department of Prints was organized to house the Museum's objects on paper. Kent was particularly concerned that the collections themselves be used, and, beginning with textiles in 1909, he organized a series of Study Rooms in the building where objects could be directly examined. This program was augmented in 1917 through the Jessie Gillender bequest: a "Study-Hours" series was initiated in which students, housewives, designers, salespeople, and even manufacturers were taught design by a trained faculty. Thus, by World War I, the Museum had developed a multifarious program in the field of applied arts.

With the election of de Forest as President in 1913, Kent was made Secretary, a position of considerable power at the Museum. The two men developed a remarkably close working relationship.[22] De Forest clearly shared Kent's populist or progressive attitudes about the Museum's mission and the importance of its educational role. As Kent later wrote, "His [de Forest's] service to the Metropolitan Museum was governed not so much by the desire to show the best art that the Museum could buy as to give the citizens of New York the benefits which might come to them through the knowledge of art and how to enjoy it."[23]

The onset of World War I proved to be a catalyst for Kent and his contemporaries. At a meeting of the New York Library Club in 1917 Kent noted, "But now the war has shut off the supply from France, and our makers of stuffs and other things are forced to see what can be done at home to provide designs for a great and 'artistic' output. . . . The designer's opportunity is at hand — provided that the museums and the libraries can help him."[24]

Many of the early leaders in this movement to get museums and libraries "outside the walls of [their] institutions" were, like Kent, trained as librarians, much influenced by the teachings of John Dewey.[25] The closing of European markets during the war prompted a decisive move by Kent into a new phase: the Museum's collections would become an alternative resource for American designers and manufacturers. Two preliminary exhibitions were held in 1915 and 1916, but in 1917 the Museum inaugurated a series of annual exhibitions of American industrial arts.[26] The Metropolitan was about to embark on what was perhaps the most ambitious program ever conceived by an American museum to promote Modern design. The next quarter century would prove to be one of the periods of greatest achievement for this institution.

1917–1925

The next twenty-three years were shaped largely by two people — Richard F. Bach and Joseph Breck — and marked by an extended relationship between the Metropolitan Museum and the American Federation of Arts (AFA), a national organization that circulated exhibitions to institutions across the country. Any museum's record of achievement may be measured in three ways: acquisitions, exhibitions — either loan shows or installations of the permanent collection — and publications. Hereafter, this essay will in large part be an assessment of the Metropolitan's record in these three areas relating to the applied arts.

The period between the world wars is perhaps best divided into two sections for discussion, as a major shift occurred in American design after the "Exposition Internationale des Arts Décoratifs et Industriels Modernes" of 1925 held in Paris. It is a complicated story involving intertwining personalities and roles.

Richard Bach was hired by the Museum in 1918 as the Associate in Industrial Arts. In the Annual Report of that year, the Trustees described his responsibilities:

> By the appointment of Richard F. Bach, Curator of the School of Architecture in Columbia University, to membership on the museum staff, the Trustees took an important step in forwarding the work with manufacturers, designers, and trade journals, a work recognized as essential now at the time of the ending of the war and all that that means to our national industries into which taste and style enter as important factors.

Mr. Bach devotes himself to the needs of manufacturers, dealers, designers, artisans, and manual craftsmen in objects of industrial art, and makes it his business to render accessible to them the resources of the collections.[27]

Bach's position was not, however, technically curatorial, so he could not make any acquisitions for the Museum; rather, he worked under Henry Kent in an educational capacity. Bach's primary duty was to direct the annual exhibitions of American industrial design. He supervised the selection of objects and the production of catalogues, and he maintained a close working relationship with manufacturers, designers, and the trade press. As Bach's reputation grew, he became a major national figure in the design field. He served on many committees and eventually was made an Associate in the Department of Industrial Arts at AFA, which led to his involving the Museum in a number of the international AFA exhibitions.

Joseph Breck returned to the Metropolitan in 1917 from a brief term at the Minneapolis Institute of Arts and assumed a joint position as Curator of Decorative Arts and Assistant Director. He was thus a major force in the Museum, and correspondence in the Museum archives shows that he ultimately influenced or made the final decisions on any significant question involving the applied arts at the Metropolitan. Breck's responsibilities were twofold. He (and his staff) were authorized to make acquisitions, and he not only bought actively from dealers but he also purchased numerous objects from the various exhibitions at the Museum. Breck was also responsible for all other modern design shows at the Metropolitan. These were of three kinds: the installation of the international exhibits done with AFA, contemporary exhibitions of foreign applied arts, and historical shows that examined the roots of Modern design. Between Bach and Breck, then, the Metropolitan had a remarkably active exhibition program, with four different types of shows held on a regular basis.

As noted, many of the exhibitions involved the American Federation of Arts, which was affiliated with the Museum primarily through two individuals. Robert de Forest, President of the Museum, was a member of the AFA board and served for a time as its president. Charles Richards, one of the most important advocates of American industrial art in the twentieth century, though now virtually forgotten, established the international AFA exhibitions; he had especially close ties to both Kent and Bach.[28] The Metropolitan Museum's role was a varied one; it might merely host a traveling exhibition or it could completely shape a show by choosing the objects, publishing the catalogue, and taking care of all registrarial responsibilities in circulating the show to other institutions.

The first design exhibitions mounted during this period by the Museum were the "annuals" of American industrial art. The purpose of these shows and the criteria for inclusion changed gradually over the years. From the beginning, however, there were several basic premises, starting with the realization that the quality of American design must be improved if it was to compete with European products. The Metropolitan was not at this point trying to alter American design radically by introducing innovative styles but was merely trying to improve the standard of current manufacturing. The Museum began to wage a campaign to convince American manufacturers that good design would sell. Although the Museum's initial commitment was to work mostly through the manufacturer, it wanted to improve the position and education of the designer in American industry. The Musée Galliera in Paris was repeatedly cited as an example. Later,

6. "1st Exhibition of Work by Manufacturers and Designers," 1917

in 1929, Henry Kent would summarize the approach worked out by the Museum:

> A dozen years ago these questions were discussed by a group of men interested in our industrial process and the training offered to the designers destined to become responsible for the artistic quality of our products, and it was resolved, after much debate, that the surest way to find the answers was to bring together examples of native-designed goods from time to time so that they could be seen and studied.[29]

In short, the Metropolitan's early annuals were to be "a cross section of the art industries."[30]

The first annual, held in 1917, was an extremely modest affair (figure 6).[31] It was installed in Classroom B — one of Kent's Study Rooms — by a Museum instructor, Robert Alan Gordon.[32] Exhibition guidelines specified that the objects had to have been made in America that year and were inspired by an object in the Metropolitan's collection. Works could be direct reproductions or simply adaptations of a form or pattern.[33] Stylistically speaking, the objects were for the most part historical revivals without much originality. It is important to note, however, that from the very beginning a wide range of material was shown, including furniture, textiles, ceramics, jewelry, drawings, costume, lighting, and photography.

The Museum realized from the start of this series the importance of the popular and trade press; the archives for the exhibitions are filled with invitations and thank-you notes sent by the Director and other staff members. Interestingly, the Metropolitan revealed itself to be remarkably open to the latest technology. The 1917 annual contained eight reels of film of "A Visit to the Metropolitan Museum of Art." Later exhibits would utilize radio and television as a means of communicating to the public.

The second annual, in 1918, was similar in organization to the previous show.[34] With the appointment of Richard Bach that year, things began to change.

The third annual showed a marked improvement.[35] The exhibit was shifted to two regular Museum galleries, as it was four times larger; this show was the first to have a published catalogue. The title — "The Museum as a Laboratory: Exhibition of Work by Manufacturers and Designers" — was perhaps most indicative of this new, activist approach. In January 1919 Bach wrote of the Museum's concerted program:

> To meet these requirements on the part of the modern manufacturing and designing world, the Metropolitan Museum maintains a large and efficient force of assistants and an extensive system of study rooms, lantern slide and photograph collections, lending collections, and other physical means of assistance. There are a number of docents or museum instructors familiar with every detail of the galleries and their contents and there is a specially trained associate [Bach, himself] whose province it is to assist in bringing together the seeker and his objective, to act as a sort of liaison officer between the Museum and the world of art in trade. This member of the staff is a person qualified to assist manufacturers and designers from the standpoint of their own requirements. He makes it his business to visit shops and workrooms, he is familiar with the processes of manufacture and keeps abreast of the market, so that he shall be able to visualize trade values in museum facilities and thus help manufacturers toward their own objectives. To this extent he becomes a field worker and an advocate of the museum militant.[36]

It was at this time that the Museum coined a number of slogans in its campaign — "to make the galleries work," "design sells," and "art into daily life" — which clearly show a reformist spirit much like that of the various European *werkbunds* of the period. Henry Kent advocated that the Metropolitan acquire objects from the annuals, but Edward Robinson, the Director, quickly rejected the idea.[37] In Richard Bach, however, Kent had finally found his protégé, and together they explored new directions for the Museum.

Like their predecessors, the exhibits of the early 1920s were more interesting in theory than in aesthetic content. The Museum's major goal at this time was to establish ties with the field of industrial design and to work out a series of guidelines for the exhibits.

For the 1920 annual there was a greater emphasis on objects currently in production rather than on custom work, an important distinction Bach would expand on in later exhibitions with his idea of "quantity production."[38] Sources of inspiration in the Museum's collection were now noted on labels. Designers, such as Elsie de Wolf, Ruth Reeves, Peer Smed, and Rafael Gustavino, began to participate alongside the manufacturers. There was, moreover, a wider variety of media shown, including packaging for toiletries, advertising, and interior-design drawings.

The fifth annual, held in 1920–21, marked the first use of the phrase "American Industrial Art" in the title.[39] Bach now began to use the term "good design" in publications, three decades before its adoption by Edgar Kaufmann, jr., for a series of contemporary design shows at the Museum of Modern Art. The fifth annual marked the

7. "The Museum of Art as a Laboratory: Sixth Exhibition of American Industrial Art," 1922

first appearance of noted architects as participants: Carrère and Hastings, John Russell Pope, and Bertram Goodhue. Such was the success of these annuals, both in New York and nationally, that participating manufacturers and department stores used the Museum's name in their advertisements.

By 1922 the sixth annual had grown to more than six hundred objects and was moved to the Gallery of Special Exhibitions (figure 7).⁴⁰ Designers' names were listed for the first time on labels, an important recognition for the profession. The Museum stipulated that objects could not have been released commercially, so that they were shown for the first time at the Metropolitan; henceforth manufacturers carefully coordinated their marketing with the Museum.

In the Annual Report the Trustees noted their approval of the Museum's accomplishments during the early 1920s as the annuals developed.

We may safely say that the foundation has been laid in the work with manufacturers and designers and the editors of their representative trade journals conducted by Mr. Bach. The stand taken by the Museum is now recognized, and the initial chapter in this phase of work has been written. From many cities the trades are now coming to the Museum; its scope is demonstrated once more as that of a national museum. . . . These exhibitions are now recognized in the trades and trade press; they are looked forward to as annual events and their example emulated.[41]

As the complexity of the shows increased, Breck formed a National Advisory Committee in 1923 to help with their organization. Committee members, however, consisted solely of manufacturers — not designers — which was still a reflection of the Museum's initial policy. Ironically, it was the seventh annual that used the word "design" for the first time in the show's title, a term that would be chosen six decades later by the Department of Twentieth Century Art for its applied arts collection.[42]

In 1924 the eighth annual — more than nine hundred objects — marked a dramatic change.[43] Three years earlier Bach had written:

Our effort has developed as part of a great movement for the benefit of American design in the industrial arts. Our exhibitions have always been representative only in small degree, since they have consisted only of things based on study in our own galleries; yet this limitation has never prevented us from offering an all-round and fairly inclusive exhibition. Were it possible to open the galleries for a general exhibition of industrial art, regardless of the source of inspiration for the motives shown, our greater effectiveness would appear at once.[44]

With the removal of this restriction, the Metropolitan became the first major museum in America to mount an annual of the best examples of contemporary design.[45] Bach no doubt was responding to the influence of Breck, who was actively acquiring and exhibiting examples of European Art Déco, new work that clearly showed how *retardataire* American design in general was at that time.

Bach, on the other hand, was thinking seriously about a new direction for American design. He was now committed to machine production as an alternative to handcraftsmanship — but within a certain context. In 1924 he wrote that "the machine cannot hurt *good* design. . . . The test of design in modern industrial art is to be found only in objects of quantity production."[46]

Industrial design or art had a different meaning in the era before World War II than it does now. Bach defined "quantity production" as "the manufacture of a number of pieces at a time from a single design, or the manufacture of a number of identical pieces from time to time, but from a model or drawings retained for the purpose."[47] It was not necessary that large numbers were produced or that objects be made completely by machine. What mattered was the intention of the designer that multiples be made in the most straightforward manner.

Bach saw this method of manufacture, moreover, as innately American. "Quantity production is a democratic expedient for getting good design to the largest number at short notice and at most reasonable cost."[48]

At the same time Bach was beginning to grapple with the issue of a contemporary style, for most of the work in the early Museum annuals had been historicizing. Like many of his European and American contemporaries, Bach was searching for a new style that would build on the past without copying it or fully breaking with it, what has been called "an intuitive rather than academic eclecticism."[49]

We have an advantage which no other era has enjoyed. The styles of all time are ours. Until we can walk freely ourselves, we lean upon these styles, meanwhile achieving a steady step and a gait and stride which will be our own. . . . Out of them and their consistent use will come that style or those styles which will represent the twentieth century.[50]

This moderate course — this search for a means to bridge the past and present — was to be indicative of the inclusive nature of the Metropolitan's collections, exhibitions, and publications then and into the future.

While Bach produced nine loan exhibitions during the pre-1925 period, Joseph Breck was involved with only two shows. The first was "Modern French Fine and Applied Art" in 1919, perhaps the first foreign showing of contemporary design at the Metropolitan Museum.[51] Although the show consisted largely of paintings and sculpture, there were also examples of ceramics, metalwork, and textiles by such artists as Auguste Delaherche and André Metthey.

Breck's second exhibit, in 1923, was devoted to "American Handicrafts."[52] It was the first collaboration between the Metropolitan Museum and the American Federation of Arts on a contemporary applied arts show, although the Museum was not involved in its preparation. The exhibition consisted of more than two hundred objects representing a wide range of media. Organized to celebrate the twenty-fifth anniversary of the famous "Arts and Crafts" exhibit in Boston (1897), the project was clearly intended to help offset the growing influence of the machine. The cause of American "craft," however, would not become an important concern for the Metropolitan until the period following World War II.[53]

Breck's major work at this time was with the permanent collection. Starting in 1922, Edward C. Moore, Jr., gave funds to the Metropolitan for the purchase of contemporary decorative arts; he was to be the first of five donors in this century who would significantly augment the twentieth-century design collection through acquisition funds or objects.[54] In 1922 Breck began to assemble the first inclusive Modern design collection in a major American museum.

Breck's taste was conservative and frankly European. Like Bach, he favored design that was part of the evolving "intuitive eclecticism." In 1927 he expressed this preference in writing about Art Déco work: "Here was beauty of proportions, of simple masses, of clean lines. . . . [T]he elements derived from the antique were so transformed that the design as a whole represented an original creation. The same freshness of expression [was achieved] without violent departure from tradition."[55] Breck's formation and exhibition of the collection during the early 1920s clearly reflected this viewpoint.

His acquisitions were largely drawn from two areas: decorative design and craft. Objects were mostly contemporary and European. There was a wide range of media — glass, ceramics (more than three dozen pieces), metalwork, textiles, architectural fragments, and furniture — although furniture was clearly considered the most important form. Remarkably, Breck's criteria would remain valid for the next sixty years.

In 1923 Breck installed a selection of his new acquisitions along with several loans from Robert de Forest's collection (figure 8). Such a seminal event in the Metropolitan's history — the first exhibition of its kind — is worthy of note. Breck chose to call the new installation "modern decorative arts."[56] The gallery was not intended to show a repre-

8. Objects acquired by Joseph Breck in 1923: commode
and mirror by Louis Süe, André Mare, and Paul Véra;
candelabra by Georg Jensen; vase by Gerhard Henning
(Purchase, Edward C. Moore, Jr., Gift, 1923: 23.175.1;
23.175.14, 23.179.1–2, 23.114.5ab)

sentative sampling of the holdings but was conceived as a rotating installation, often incorporating new acquisitions.[57] Breck clearly envisioned the new gallery as a space to show what had happened in Europe and what was to come in America.

Today, after a decade ripe with promise, there is every indication that we are to see in our own time the triumph of a modern style, based on tradition but modified, as this perilous inheritance has always been modified in every great period of the past, to meet the new requirements of changed conditions of life. In France, Germany, Austria, and other European countries, the development of a modern style in the field of the applied arts is taking place so rapidly that the International Exposition of Decorative Arts, to be held in Paris in 1924 [*sic*], should definitely mark the beginning of a new era.

If the decorative arts in Europe are speedily outgrowing the period of tutelage characterized by the copy and the pastiche, this country has contributed little as yet to the evolution of a new style. The dependence on the past, which characterizes so much of our applied art today, would be disheartening were it not, as we confidently believe, merely a stage in the evolution of taste — a period of assimilation which will be followed in due time by one of original expression. In matters of art we learn from the past; but, apprentice days over, we must make our own contribution to the living tradition of art. That such contributions have been made during the last fifty years, and are becoming increasingly more numerous, is evident even in the little collection now displayed, and justifies the Museum in its venture into this uncharted domain.[58]

The installation quite naturally reflected the variety of material in the collection, but it was the chronological range of objects that was exceptional. Two generations of American and European artists were shown spanning the decades from about 1870 to 1923. Stylistically, the gallery included both Art Déco and Art Nouveau — the latter being then much out of vogue. Once again, Breck's vision proved perceptive, for both of these styles have remained a strength of the Metropolitan's holdings down to the present.

Thus, by 1925, both Bach and Breck had established their positions at the Museum. After nine annuals, Bach had finally changed the format of the exhibitions and clarified his own thinking. With funding behind him, Breck had begun the formation of a Modern design collection, which was placed on view for the American public and designers. It is particularly important to note that all of this had been accomplished *before* the Paris Exposition of 1925. During the next fifteen years, the Metropolitan's program would expand even more dramatically.

1925–1940

Although Modern design and architecture existed in the United States before 1925, the Paris Exposition that year had a considerable impact in this country, particularly in the applied arts.[59] Perhaps more than anything else, the Exposition made Americans aware that Modern design was still very much a nascent movement here. During the late 1920s, there was a virtual explosion of interest in such innovative work by American designers, critics, department stores, and museums. The Metropolitan proved to be one of the most influential leaders in the field.

Among Joseph Breck's most important undertakings was a series of exhibitions of contemporary applied arts from abroad. In 1926, while Breck was Acting Director, the Metropolitan hosted an exhibit of material from the Paris Exposition selected by Charles Richards for the American Association of Museums (AAM). The range of Western design was international — except for Germany and the United States, which had not participated — but stylistically the work was quite conservative. Only Art Déco objects (figure 9) were chosen, even though Modernist and moderne design had been shown in Paris. Nonetheless, this 1926 exhibit was immensely influential, for its nine-city tour gave many Americans their first exposure to this new style. Breck himself wrote of the Exposition's importance.

For the past twenty-five years and more a new style in decoration has been developing in Europe. It has thrown overboard the copy and the pastiche which the topsy-turvy nineteenth century in the throes of industrialism substituted for orig-

9. Exhibition of selected objects from the 1925 Paris Exposition, 1926

inal creation. It strives to embody old principles in new forms of beauty, and to meet new conditions of living with frankness and understanding. The "historic styles" were not created overnight, and, doubtless, considerable time must elapse before this "modern style" takes definite shape. But that it has already attained international proportions; that it has the adherence of many of the leading European manufacturers and artists in the field of decorative art; that it is profoundly influencing the education of the younger generation of artists; that it has won the suffrage of a wide public; and finally, that work in this new style is already being produced which equals in beauty the achievements of any age, were demonstrated beyond question in the great Paris exposition of 1925, devoted exclusively to decorative arts in the modern spirit.[60]

Two further points should be noted about the AAM exhibit. A number of objects by major designers were grouped in ensembles. This was a significant departure for the Metropolitan in installation technique, and it would serve as a precedent for Bach's shows in the late 1920s and 1930s. Also, the Paris Exposition was of special interest to Breck since he had made a number of major acquisitions in France during 1925; these objects were on view concurrently with the 1926 exhibit.

One of France's rivals as a leader in the applied arts during the period before World War II was Sweden. In 1927 the Museum hosted a large exhibition of contemporary Swedish decorative arts, the first in a series of Scandinavian shows held at the Metropolitan.[61] Nordic design appealed to Museum officials and the American public because it was thought to be less aristocratic and more democratic. Breck noted that

10. "Swedish Contemporary Decorative Arts," 1927

"contemporary Swedish decorative art is far from expensive or luxurious in character. It reflects, on the contrary, the tastes and needs of the comfortable middle class for which it is made."[62]

The exhibit itself (figure 10) was designed by Carl G. Bergsten, the architect of the Swedish Pavilion at the Paris Exposition, and it was a marked improvement over the Museum's usual installations.[63] This appears to be the first instance in which the Metropolitan allowed a noted artist to design a contemporary exhibit in the Museum, and it too would serve as a model for Bach. Breck was so taken with Swedish design that he purchased thirteen pieces of glass from the exhibit.[64]

A third international exhibition, held in 1930, was devoted to Mexican fine and applied arts from the sixteenth century to the present.[65] The show was organized by René d'Harnoncourt for AFA and included historic and contemporary applied arts — both craft and folk art. Like the "American Handicrafts" exhibit of 1923, this show was one of the few in which the Museum ventured away from its commitment to industrial art during the prewar period.

Perhaps the most lasting aspect of a curator's work is acquisitions. Joseph Breck left a small, but remarkably fine, collection of modern design at the Metropolitan.[66] He began to acquire Art Nouveau and Art Déco design in 1922, and he augmented this collection significantly three years later with a number of items purchased in Paris at the time of the Exposition (see pages 156–77). Among the more notable Art Déco examples were a cabinet by Jacques Émile Ruhlmann, an armchair and desk by Süe et Mare, and a silver service by Jean Puiforcat.[67] In 1926 Breck bought some examples of French Art Nouveau ceramics and furniture, including an armchair by Georges de Feure (figure 11);

11. Armchair, 1899–1900, by Georges de Feure. Purchase, Edward C. Moore, Jr., Gift, 1926 (26.228.2)

12. Cabinet, 1861, by Philip Webb for Morris and Company. Rogers Fund, 1926 (26.26.54)

many of these objects were purchased from Samuel Bing's famous shop, L'Art Nouveau. In the previous year, the Museum had acquired a number of objects by Louis Tiffany on extended loan from the Tiffany Foundation.[68] Breck was keenly aware of the roots of Modern design, and in 1926 he also purchased a remarkable English Arts and Crafts cabinet by Philip Webb (figure 12). Three years later several examples of Danish and French ceramics were acquired.[69]

In 1926 a gallery in the Museum was opened for "the display of the permanent collection of modern decorative arts. Up to then the collection had been shown in a small gallery in a distant part of the Museum."[70] Located next to the Gallery of Special Exhibitions, this was the first prominent and long-term space allotted to Modern design at the Metropolitan. It is not clear how long the gallery was maintained, although photographs of it exist as late as 1929 (figure 13), and there are references to it in the *Bulletin* of January 1935.

It is worth noting what Breck meant by "modern" in 1926. As in his temporary exhibition of 1923, the installation consisted of decorative design and craft, and the chronological range spanned approximately a half century. Writing of a new acquisition, Breck also noted the criteria that he thought of as "characteristic of the recent trend in furniture design": "the absence of ornament," an emphasis on the inherent qualities of the material, and "the carefully studied proportions of . . . simple forms."[71] Theoretically at least, Breck's ideas sounded remarkably like the Modernists' with the exception of their insistence on asymmetrical, planar forms (see page 106). This moderate stance thus allowed the Metropolitan to collect a wide variety of contemporary work.

13. The Modern Decorative Arts Gallery, photographed in 1929

The third aspect of Breck's responsibilities involved the historical shows mounted by the Department of Decorative Arts, which generally consisted of three types. These exhibitions were by no means the large-scale art historical shows that we have become accustomed to since World War II. Although the Museum mounted innumerable contemporary exhibitions, it could not at this point deal with the Modern Movement in any kind of significant historical context.

The first type of exhibition included "one-medium" shows that drew primarily on the Museum's permanent collections. The earliest, held in 1927, was "Painted and Printed Fabrics," with approximately twenty American, French, and English textiles.[72] The second of these exhibits (1936) mounted by the Decorative Arts Department was devoted to glass from 1500 B.C. to the present.[73] It enabled the Museum to display a number of new acquisitions from Steuben, but even more important was the fact that it afforded a much-needed opportunity to show modern work in an historical perspective in terms of form, material, and technique.

The second category of exhibit involved three "one-man" shows, extremely modest affairs devoted to American artists represented in the collection:[74] Adelaide Alsop Robineau (1929–30), Charles F. Binns (1935), and John La Farge (1936).[75] The first two were memorial shows done shortly after the ceramists had died; the third was a centennial celebration of La Farge's birth. The two ceramic exhibits are of interest for they mark the beginnings of C. Louise Avery's impact on the Department of Decorative Arts; she would be largely responsible for shaping the ceramics collection, even into the 1950s.[76]

Finally, there was an exhibition of Victorian and Edwardian dresses, held in 1939.[77] Although the installation consisted of only sixty examples, this seems to have been the first show devoted to modern costume, a harbinger of what would be a major focus of the Museum after the Second World War.

Departments at the Metropolitan often reflect the personalities of their senior curators in terms of structure and ambition. Nowhere was this truer than with Joseph Breck and the significant mandate that he exercised at the Museum. After his death in 1933, the Department of Decorative Arts was divided into three parts: Medieval Art, The American Wing (objects from European colonization to 1825), and Renaissance and Modern Art (including American art after 1825). This marked the first use of the term "modern" for a department at the Metropolitan. With Preston Remington as the new head, the department continued to make acquisitions, although not with Bach's scope.[78] In 1934, for example, the Museum acquired a number of pieces of French and Danish moderne design, including metalwork, glass, and ceramics.[79]

Richard Bach's work at the Museum during the fifteen years before World War II had an immediate impact on the field. He continued the remarkable series of annuals of American industrial art, but he was also involved with Breck in the organization of three shows with AFA.

In 1926 Bach wrote to Henry Kent with a proposal for a series of American "one-line" (i.e., material) or "one-man" exhibitions at the Museum; he cited the Musée Galliera in Paris as the model and included a checklist of their shows from 1901 through 1926.[80] Shortly thereafter the General Education Board, through Charles Richards, made a grant to AFA for three international one-material exhibits.[81] A Department of Industrial Art was established within AFA with Richard Bach and Helen Plumb as associates. Bach and Plumb coordinated with advisory committees in each country, and their preliminary selections were then judged by an American jury appointed by AFA. The shows were installed at the Metropolitan by the Department of Decorative Arts, which occasionally made acquisitions from the exhibits. Given such an elaborate and ambitious structure, it is amazing that these large exhibitions were often mounted within a year's time.

In essence, Richards conceived of these shows as a way "to bring to the American public and to American manufacturers, merchants and designers the best foreign achievements in a particular field of applied art side by side with our own creations in the hope that thus we may be able more readily to estimate our own position and to take advantage of whatever suggestions the contemporary work of other peoples may hold for us."[82] The exhibitions were envisioned as having a national impact, much like the large expositions in the second half of the nineteenth century. Louise Avery wrote that "they serve a similar purpose. By reaching thousands of Americans through their display in seven or eight of the most important museums in this country, they will have tremendous appeal."[83] The shows were limited to contemporary Western European and American work but included the entire range of decorative and industrial design, as well as craft. Because they were organized by media, the emphasis was generally on new materials or techniques. Objects were usually grouped by country, and points were often made about national characteristics or trends to compare with American production.

The first exhibit, in 1928, was devoted to ceramics.[84] It included functional and sculptural pieces, as well as architectural work, a division that would become much more pronounced in post-1960 ceramics. There was, in fact, little Modernist work in this initial exhibit (figure 14).

In the next year the subject was glass and rugs.[85] Americans were now becoming aware of the growing schism in Europe between handmade and machine production, often with nationalistic overtones. Louise Avery noted:

14. "International Exhibition of Ceramic Art,"
1928

15. The tenth industrial art annual, 1926

It is interesting to contrast prevailing trends in French and German craftsmanship and to discover the services performed by each. Despite unfavorable conditions, France has continued to support artists who, working individually, produce pieces of unique character. There are many of these artists, like Décorchemont and Marinot, who, though they can never serve a large public, nevertheless fashion pieces of first rank, such as collectors will treasure highly, and who undoubtedly exert tremendous influence upon less creative artists. It is this quality in the French temperament which has always made France an originator and arbiter of styles. In Germany, poverty has strengthened the natural tendency to be intensely practical and to stress simplicity and utility. Consequently here we find a great demand for things of good design, extremely simple in form and decoration, which can be produced in factories in large quantity and sold at small cost. The Federation's present exhibition of modern rugs and glassware illustrates both these extremes and also many intermediate variations.[86]

In 1930 the third, and final, AFA collaboration was devoted to metalwork and cotton textiles, the latter chosen because it constituted such a large part of the American textile industry.[87] Richards himself seems to have been aware of an increased interest in Modernism in America and spoke supportively of this new design aesthetic.

This emphasis upon functional design and suppression of ornament is reflected today in all the countries of western continental Europe, but in varying degree, according to the temper of the different peoples....
One sometimes feels that the principle of functional design has been so studiously followed that all considerations of agreeable contours, interest of surface,

and elegance of effect are ruthlessly set aside with results that are often harsh and uncompromising. In other words, we seem to be in danger of the distressing results of art by formula. This may be true, but one must realize that we are in a state of transition and flux in the matter of contemporary design, and that it behooves us to judge these experiments leniently with the thought that they represent a sound and sane initial approach to the problem of design for the machine and constitute a basis that will in time, we may well hope, rescue us from the endless repetition of forms and ornament based on outworn traditions of hand craftsmanship.

It is the Germans who have carried this idea farthest. With characteristic zeal, they are concentrating upon the effort to produce "type forms" in which both the limitations and capabilities of the machine are recognized and which can be produced with the greatest speed and economy.[88]

The exhibition, in fact, included a number of textiles and metalwork from the Bauhaus at Dessau. The Metropolitan was thus among the earliest museums in the United States to debate and exhibit Modernist design, although, sadly, it failed to acquire any objects from these significant exhibitions.[89] The Museum's commitment during these decades was primarily to decorative design, as Bach's annuals made evident.

In 1924 Bach had finally persuaded the Museum to change the criteria for inclusion from objects inspired by the Metropolitan's collection to the best examples of American design. It was not until two years later — in the tenth annual — that he achieved his real goal: the display of original design rather than the historicizing work seen earlier.[90] The rules for the annual of 1926–27 excluded reproductions and further required that objects could not have been exhibited previously. One of the most notable pieces in the show was a large table made by John Helmsky, Inc., reflecting an Americanized version of Art Déco (figure 15).

The Museum during these years had an active collaboration not only with AFA but also with a number of department stores in New York.[91] Perhaps the most significant was with Macy's, which mounted two large exhibits in 1927 and 1928.[92] Richard Bach was involved with both, as was Robert de Forest. For the opening of the "Exposition of Art in Trade at Macy's" in 1927, de Forest, as President of the Museum, made two very important points concerning contemporary applied arts that reflected his populist viewpoint:

> Until recently most people thought of art museums only in terms of painting and sculpture. It was the Germans, as I recall, who first began to admit to their art exhibitions objects of applied or industrial art. These objects were classed in their catalogues under the heading of "Kleine Kunste" — the small arts. I have always resented this classification; it was treating the arts which must enter into the life of the people and the home with indignity. This attitude toward industrial art, which was by no means confined to the Germans, has now changed. The small arts have come into their own.
>
> All of our principal American art museums today are collecting and exhibiting objects of industrial art, and the once small arts are given a place of honor on an equality with the fine arts of painting and sculpture.
>
> The last great Paris art exhibition was in fact limited to industrial art, and it is

16. The court designed by Armistead Fitzhugh for the Museum's eleventh industrial art annual, 1929

17. Bedroom designed by John Wellborn Root for the 1929 annual

notable that among the most important exhibits of this great international exhibition in the art center of the world were those of the four great department stores of Paris, thus emphasizing what we are emphasizing today — the relation of the department store to the development of art. . . .

Our great department stores . . . exert an even wider influence than our own art museums. They not only show, but they circulate — they give the opportunity not only of seeing but of buying, taking away, and bringing into the home.[93]

The Macy's exhibition of 1927 was planned by Lee Simonson, and it included a number of contemporary group settings by noted American designers such as Paul Frankl and Jules Bouy. The 1928 show was international in scope, with room settings by such Europeans as Bruno Paul, Josef Hoffmann, and Gio Ponti, and such American designers as Eugene Schoen, Kem Weber, and William Lescaze. Of particular interest was Simonson's layout of the exhibit, which featured a central court with fountain, around which the room settings and cases for small objects were arranged.

Thus by the eleventh annual in 1929, the situation in the design field had changed dramatically for Bach. Joseph Breck had exhibited some of the most advanced Modern design from Europe on the one hand, while New York department stores had gone further in showing complete room settings. Bach responded by radically altering the concept of the annuals. He formed a new Cooperating Committee, which consisted of some of the most noted architects in America, instead of manufacturers. The title of the exhibition was correspondingly changed to "The Architect and the Industrial Arts." The show featured thirteen room settings — both domestic and commercial — designed by nine architects, and all of the objects were created especially for the occasion.[94] The

18. Dining room designed by Eliel Saarinen for the 1929 annual

19. Office designed by Raymond Hood for the 1929 annual

importance of the 1929 annual was, of course, that the Metropolitan was at long last moving away from didactic shows like the early annuals and the AFA collaborations toward the active promotion of a new, modern style. The eleventh annual remains perhaps the epitome of the American version of Art Déco.

The organization of the exhibition was done by the architects working together. The general layout of the gallery was completed by Eliel Saarinen, although the central court with fountain was designed by Armistead Fitzhugh (figure 16). Two interesting proposals were never realized: Frank Lloyd Wright was asked to submit a music room, and Eliel Saarinen was to have designed an "automobile exhibit" for the central garden.[95] Even as executed, however, the eleventh annual proved to be a diverse exhibition illustrating three directions in Art Déco during the late 1920s. A number of the settings were clearly influenced by French work, such as the bedroom by John Wellborn Root (figure 17). In contrast, other rooms were highly geometric in terms of form and patterning, as in the dining room by Eliel Saarinen (figure 18). Lastly, there were interiors that anticipated the moderne with their emphasis on metal and glass, most notably the executive's office by Raymond Hood (figure 19).

The twelfth exhibit, in 1931, marked a return by Bach to the earlier format of the annuals, with a didactic installation showing the current state of manufacturing.[96] One notable change was the inclusion of a new generation of artists — the industrial designer, an American invention. In the introduction to the exhibition catalogue Bach wrote at length about his view of contemporary design: its determinants, terminology, and evolution. Clearly, he was still grappling with the exact role that the Museum should play in such a burgeoning movement. "The position of The Metropolitan Museum of Art with regard to contemporary industrial art is that of recorder and demonstrator, possibly also that of qualified observer. It assumes no authority, declines the power of arbitrator."[97] This moderate stance was in sharp contrast to that of a museum that had just emerged as a dynamic force in the contemporary field.

In 1929 the Museum of Modern Art had been founded, in many ways as a protest against the conservatism of American museums, including the Metropolitan. Four years later, MoMA sponsored its first design show, "Modern Architecture: International Exhibition," which was organized by Henry-Russell Hitchcock and Philip Johnson. In 1933 a Department of Architecture was established, with Johnson as its twenty-seven-year-old chairman. Among Johnson's earliest exhibits were "Objects: 1900 and Today" (1933) and "Machine Art" (1934).[98] Alfred Barr and Johnson formulated an approach in the early 1930s that stood in marked contrast to the Metropolitan. MoMA focused primarily on one style, Modernism, and its historical roots, assuming an almost evangelical spirit in its commitment to what it saw as the avant-garde. Its stance, moreover, became an exclusive one — in contrast to the Metropolitan's inclusive, moderate approach — especially in MoMA's tendency toward European rather than American design. Architecture and the applied arts were to receive equal emphasis, particularly in terms of exhibitions and publications, while the Metropolitan's commitment was clearly to the applied arts. In the collecting of applied arts, MoMA's emphasis was on industrial design; craft and decorative design were of secondary importance, the latter almost to the point of exclusion.

At the start of a new decade, Bach's position was thus a delicate one, as he was confronted on all sides — department stores, designers' groups, and other museums — with an enormous amount of activity. In 1934 his office was restructured, no doubt as part of the general reorganization at the Metropolitan that resulted from the breakup of the Department of Decorative Arts after Breck's death. A Department of Industrial Relations had been created in 1928, but its responsibilities were now considerably augmented. Study Hours — now renamed Study Hours in Color and Design — were placed in Bach's department; their educational programs were dramatically expanded for students, professionals in the field, and the general public. A new division called Neighborhood Circulating Exhibitions was created to make the Museum's collections available to other areas in the city. A wide variety of programs was organized for "satellite" museums around the boroughs; the program proved to be immensely popular and drew hundreds of thousands of visitors until its cessation in 1941. But it was in terms of exhibitions that Bach was to have his most dramatic impact in the field.

For the thirteenth annual, in 1934–35 (figure 20), Bach returned to his format of room settings first used in 1929.[99] The opulence of the Art Déco style had ended with the Depression, and by the early 1930s American designers were searching for a new aesthetic — the moderne (see page 178) — which would reflect the economic, technological, and political reality of the New Deal. The Chicago World's Fair of 1933 was perhaps the first mass display of this new design approach.[100] Bach's annual the next year clearly reflected a major shift toward "quantity production." One of the participating designers noted the Committee's middle-class approach:

> The Co-operating Committee agreed that in contradistinction to the exhibition held in the lush period of five years ago, this one was to show what might be achieved at a low cost. As a gauge it was felt that any article put into mass production must be within the digestive capacity of the pocketbooks of those who paid

20. "Contemporary American Industrial Art," 1934　　　　21. "Room for a Lady" designed by Eliel Saarinen for the 1934 annual

on an average of say twenty dollars per room per month. While we may still "love the garish day" we welcome any opportunity to try to create a fine thing in a simple manner.[101]

The show clearly found a favorable response with the public, for the thirteenth annual was the most widely attended exhibition to have been held at the Metropolitan Museum. The committee, in fact, consisted of two generations of artists: twenty architects and industrial designers. The team of architects was given the central gallery under the direction of Arthur Loomis Harmon; the two younger groups of industrial designers were assigned the end galleries and were directed by Ely Jacques Kahn and Paul Philippe Cret.[102]

Perhaps no annual so clearly reflected Bach's inclusive approach to contemporary industrial art. Many of the older architects, who had participated in the 1929 exhibit, returned. Eliel Saarinen's "Room for a Lady" (figure 21) is indicative of their attempt to absorb a new aesthetic: the use of built-in seating and storage; the move to painted wood finishes to achieve sleek, polished surfaces; and a considerably more restrained use of geometric pattern and ornament. The work of industrial designers, such as Donald Deskey's dining room, contrasted markedly in their use of glass for mirrors, shelves, windows, and walls; metal for structural frames, lighting, and ornamental trim; and especially in the use of the "streamlined" curve. The "Designer's Office and Studio" by Raymond Loewy and Lee Simonson (figure 22) became one of the most famous American moderne interiors of the 1930s. Even the American Modernists were represented in William Lescaze's living room (figure 23): the absence of any ornamentation, the planar walls of plaster and glass, the built-in lighting and furniture, and the tubular-steel armchair are all representative of this International Style.

By 1934, however, the schism between the advocates of industrial and decorative

22. Office designed by Raymond Loewy and
Lee Simonson for the 1934 annual

23. Living room designed by William Lescaze for the 1934 annual

design had become even more pronounced, with the two major museums in New York being increasingly cast in adversarial roles. Lewis Mumford in his "Sky Line" column in *The New Yorker* noted:

> Except in details, the exhibition now at the Metropolitan Museum is marking time. There has been no substantial advance over the forms that were on view five years ago.
> What is lacking in this exhibition is at least one modest room, composed of run-of-the-mill products, such as Mr. Philip Johnson recently showed at the Museum of Modern Art. That would be an object lesson in the grand fact that with the machine, beauty does not hinge upon expense. In its present form, the exhibition hardly differs seriously enough from that of a good department store to warrant the Metropolitan's special efforts.[103]

Richard Bach was to find that moderation was not always a virtue. In 1937 Bach, at the age of fifty, proposed a new series of industrial art shows that he hoped would reassert the Museum's position and extend well into the 1940s.[104] The Metropolitan would mount four types of exhibitions on an alternating basis: comprehensive shows including all kinds of applied arts (the industrial art annuals), one-material shows limited to American products, international one-material exhibits, and historical shows.

The first of the one-material shows of American design was the fourteenth annual in 1937.[105] It was a small exhibition devoted to silver, and it included both handmade and industrially manufactured objects, although the material was decidedly decorative. Forty pieces from the exhibit were shown in the United States Pavilion at the Paris Exposition in 1937.

That same year the first international one-material show was devoted to rugs and carpets.[106] Like the silver exhibit, the installation included handcrafted and machine-made products; but both of the exhibitions lacked an aesthetic focus, since they were envisioned as overviews of the field. Of particular interest was a suggestion by Bach in 1936 that the Museum, in conjunction with the exhibition, should sponsor a competition with a carpet association to manufacture the winners. This idea would be developed by the Museum of Modern Art in two competitions in 1940–41 and 1948.[107]

By the time of the fifteenth annual, in 1940, a pronounced reaction had set in against the machine aesthetics — both Modernism and the moderne — showing a definite shift toward organic and biomorphic design with an emphasis on irregular form, texture, and nature.[108] One of the most perceptive critics of the period, Elizabeth Mock, noted:

> What gives the Museum's exhibition its importance is its faithful reflection of the newest tendencies in design. . . . If Mr. John Doe drops in to see the exhibition of Contemporary American Industrial Art which the Metropolitan Museum is showing this summer, he will doubtless be pleased to find that fashion has swung away from the functionalist design which he has always found so forbidding.[109]

The estrangement from such "functionalist" design had become so decided that Mock was led to remark further that "applied art had probably never been so inaccessible to its intended public."

The Cooperating Committee for the exhibition consisted of twenty-two artists — twelve architects and ten designers — who produced thirteen domestic room settings under the general direction of Ely Jacques Kahn. A few of the first generation from the 1929 exhibit returned, such as Eugene Schoen, Ralph Walker, and Kahn. It was, however, a younger generation that dominated the fifteenth annual, one that consisted of industrial designers — Donald Deskey, Russel Wright, and Gilbert Rohde — and architects — Wallace Harrison, Edward Durell Stone, and Louis Skidmore.[110]

The new interiors showed a marked contrast to the sleek moderne settings created six years earlier. A "Dining Alcove" by Stone (figure 24) put a heavy emphasis on texture in its use of grass matting, exposed brick walls, bamboo lattice, and undulating wood ceiling. More sophisticated was Wallace Harrison's "Hall of a Country House" (figure 25), a fanciful play of the functional and decorative. The freestanding closet and wash basin were exposed as major elements in the design; walls were covered in geometric wood paneling, against which the architect contrasted myriad biomorphic shapes in the carpeting, the furniture, a suspended ceiling panel, and even a mobile by Alexander Calder. A living room by Gilbert Rohde (figure 26) showed a similar emphasis on irregular forms and textures.

In addition to the room settings, there were also auxiliary displays worthy of note:

> New materials are employed and new methods of utilizing old materials — fabrics of glass, fluorescent-tube lighting, plastics of recent development, new treatments of metals, and new methods of applying glass to walls, to mention only a few. There are four groups arranged by material; these consist of metals, glass, plastic, ceramics, synthetic fabrics, and wood.[111]

Perhaps the most interesting exhibit was "Metals and Synthetic Textiles" by Louis

24. Dining room designed by Edward Durell Stone for the 1940 annual

25. "Hall of a Country House" designed by Wallace K. Harrison for the 1940 annual

Skidmore and Harvey Wiley Corbett (figure 27). It was a dramatic architectural installation consisting of a free-form base, a cantilevered aluminum structure with stainless-steel wires, gooseneck lamps for lighting, and a floating, curved canopy.

The 1940 exhibit was to be the last of the annuals, although Bach did not realize this at the time. The onset of the Second World War severely curtailed the Museum's activities, but afterward the institution entered a new phase under another director. A remarkable quarter century of achievement in the field of contemporary design had come to an end.

1940—1967

It is not clear why the Metropolitan Museum withdrew during the 1940s from an active role in Modern design. Certainly, a deliberate decision to do so would have involved discussions between the Director and the staff, yet no evidence seems to exist in the Museum's archives. In 1952 Richard Bach wrote simply that "re-deployment of Museum staff and assignments in relation to the War and the disturbed situation following, both in the Museum and in industry, combined to discourage their resumption."[112]

It is true that major changes had occurred in the Museum's staff, even as early as the 1930s. Two design advocates — Robert de Forest and Joseph Breck — had died in 1931 and 1933, respectively, but perhaps the most serious loss was the retirement of Henry Kent in 1940.[113] He had wielded enormous power at the Museum and was the one who had first conceived the industrial art shows. The year after he left, the Department of Industrial Relations was disbanded, and Bach was made Dean of an enlarged Department of Education and Extension, a position he held until 1949.

The most dramatic change at the Metropolitan was undoubtedly the arrival in 1940 of Francis Henry Taylor, one of the youngest and most mercurial directors to serve the

26. Living room designed by Gilbert Rohde for the 1940 annual

27. Display designed by Louis Skidmore and Harvey Wiley Corbett
for the 1940 annual

Museum. In the Annual Report that year Taylor wrote supportively of the Museum's record in the field of contemporary design, placing a particular emphasis on fashion and textiles.

> With the collapse of Paris as the fashion center of the world, New York has become the market not merely of the Western Hemisphere but, certainly so far as the luxury trades are concerned, the only large free exchange operating at the present time. The Museum has within its walls, in its collections of textiles, prints, and decorative arts, the most comprehensive body of study material on this continent. And all of this, taken in consideration with the collections of documents on ornament in the Print Department, places this institution in the front ranks of all the museums of the world as a source for students and designers. One of the most important and immediate functions of the Museum is to place this material at the disposal of industry and to take its proper part in the commercial as well as intellectual life of the city.[114]

In 1940 Bach prepared a report for the Trustees proposing an ambitious program of exhibitions:

> I visualize as part of a general program of industrial art exhibitions not only the comprehensive and the one-material types, but also large shows held outside the building under our direction, but with the cooperation of other museums in the city. Such exhibitions would contain not only complete room schemes, in full scale, consisting entirely of specially designed products, but also related displays of materials and processes, and products to illustrate them.[115]

No written record exists of Taylor's response to Bach's memo, but within a year relations between the two men seem to have become strained.[116] Perhaps it was the difference in their ages — Bach was fifty-three, Taylor thirty-seven — or the fact that Bach had so clearly been one of Kent's protégés for twenty-two years. Whatever the reason, it became evident early in Taylor's tenure that Bach's programs would not be renewed.

From a curatorial point of view, the situation was even more disheartening. There was no single individual now in charge of the modern collection, nor was there any master plan for acquisitions. Objects continued to come into the collection during this quarter century, although in a random manner. To some degree, this was the result of a repeated reorganization of the decorative arts departments after Breck's death in 1933. The American Wing was initially limited to objects dating before 1825, so that all later material would have been collected by the Department of Renaissance and Modern Art. It is not clear at what point the wing was given responsibility for all American decorative arts, but it definitely occurred before a further shifting of departments by Taylor in 1948, when he created a new division called American Art, which combined the fine and applied arts.[117]

The situation became even more confused in the next decade with the appointment of James J. Rorimer as Director in 1955. All the American and European departments were realigned the following year, but the Modern design holdings were still split into European and American divisions, thus preventing any kind of coherent collecting.[118]

The other major curatorial change in the post-1940 period was the arrival of the Costume Institute at the Metropolitan. The collection had initially been formed by Irene and Alice Lewisohn in the early twentieth century, but it was not organized as a museum until 1937. Although it became a part of the Metropolitan seven years later, the Costume Institute did not move there until 1946, and it would be thirteen years more before it was made a curatorial department.[119]

The Museum had collected costumes before 1944 as part of its textile holdings, and a number of exhibitions had been mounted (see Appendix A). The addition of the Costume Institute, however, was portentous for the Museum's involvement with the entire design field. Taylor had shown the Lewisohn collection in 1937 while he was still Director of the Worcester Art Museum, and as Director of the Metropolitan he negotiated its transference there, where he envisioned it as a major resource for the field. In 1945 the Trustees noted their approval of the transaction.

> The most distinguished of our moves in the direction of assistance to industry has been in our alliance with the Costume Institute. Under the highly able management of Miss Dorothy Shaver, this organization in 1944 became a part of the Metropolitan Museum. Its collections are now to be moved to our halls, and we are planning a most active use of them as examples in matters of taste and design. Members of the fashion industry, both corporate and individual, have contributed largely to the funds necessary to carry on the Institute. We hope to establish an active, living relationship with the industry by consultation with those who are directly interested in the organization.
>
> In furtherance of our charter purpose of "encouraging and developing . . . the application of arts to manufacture and practical life," the Trustees have this year created several classes of industrial membership open to all corporations, associa-

28. Dress, ca. 1945, by Adrian, exhibited in
"American Fashions and Fabrics," 1945

tions, and partnerships. We have had a fine initial response from industrial
contributors, which should and will grow as more industries become aware of the
unparalleled sources of design and the wealth of reference material available at the
Museum.[120]

In 1946 Taylor himself wrote, "A major accomplishment of the year here under review was
the union of the Costume Institute with the Museum. This was not only a benefit to
both institutions but a long, forward step on the part of the Museum in the large field of
industrial relations."[121]

Under the leadership of Polaire Weissman, the Costume Institute became a
dynamic department at the Museum in terms of acquisitions and exhibitions (figure 28).
It initially produced one or two shows a year, and, with the establishment of the "Party of
the Year" benefit in 1948, the Institute became a major force in the world of couture, with
strong ties to designers and manufacturers. Its annual exhibitions, moreover, had a
substantial impact on the design world, particularly after the appointment of Diana
Vreeland in 1972.[122]

Whether by design or osmosis, a profound change began to occur at the
Metropolitan by the late 1940s. The Museum's commitment to "the application of arts to
manufacture and practical life" shifted from the applied arts (i.e., decorative design, craft,
and industrial design) to costume. In terms of publications and exhibitions — although
not acquisitions — the applied arts would be unable, in the second half of the twentieth
century, to regain the preeminent position at the Museum they had had in the days of
Bach and Breck.

29. "Modern British Crafts," 1942

During the 1940s Edgar Kaufmann, jr., would in many ways become Richard Bach's successor, though at the Museum of Modern Art. He made MoMA an international leader in the field of industrial design, and his design policy has been largely retained to the present. The removal of the Metropolitan as a moderating influence in the applied arts no doubt contributed in part to the ascendance of Modernism as the predominant style in America during the postwar years. The Museum did not completely abandon the field, for it hosted a number of exhibits during this quarter century, but it was not as actively involved in their organization as in the prewar years.

Most of the shows were in fact devoted to craft, and Bach was initially involved with several of these exhibits. From the late 1930s, his interest had begun to shift from industrial art to craft, and he worked with Aileen Osborn Webb on committees for national surveys, competitions, and exhibitions, for what would eventually become the American Craft Council and Museum; this work extended at least into the early 1950s.[123] Bach's views on what constituted craft are particularly interesting. Consistent with his inclusive definition of industrial art, craft did not necessarily exclude the machine. In fact, much debate was given during this period to the terms "craftsman/designer" and "designer/craftsman."

One of the first visual demonstrations of Bach's view of craft was an exhibit held in 1942 of "Modern British Crafts," which he helped to organize.[124] Most of the work was quite conservative and consisted of what we would now call folk and decorative art (figure 29). Charles Marriott, an English critic, noted the peculiar position of the machine in British design at that time: "The crux of the present situation in British crafts is the existence side by side of hand and machine production. . . . Wisely for its purpose the exhibition has been limited for the most part to handicrafts and works in which the machine is not more than an adjunct."[125]

The Museum's next mixed-media exhibit was held in 1952 in collaboration with Webb's group, the American Craftsmen's Educational Council.[126] The traveling show, which comprised more than two hundred objects, was assembled at the request of the Department of State to give an international audience an overview of contemporary American handicrafts.

Of considerably more interest was a series of single-medium exhibits done after the Second World War. These shows were successors to the one-material exhibits organized before 1940. The first was held in 1947 and consisted of some 250 examples of contemporary ceramics selected from the Eleventh Ceramic National Exhibition sponsored by the Syracuse Museum of Fine Art.[127] Richard Bach served as chairman of the national jury, and many leaders in the postwar American ceramics field were included: Arthur Baggs, Maija Grotell, Viktor Schreckengost, Marguerite Wildenhain, and Beatrice Wood.

In 1959 the Museum hosted an international show of some 350 examples of American, Canadian, and European work drawn from the XX Ceramic International.[128] The Metropolitan mounted at the same time two supplementary shows, one of forty historical ceramics from its own collection and the other of contemporary American work purchased since 1922. The main exhibit, coordinated by Carl Dauterman in the Department of Renaissance and Post-Renaissance Art, consisted of "wheel-turned" (i.e., functional) vessels and sculptural ceramics, though not industrially manufactured objects.[129] At this early date Dauterman noted a major new development in the craft field — the emergence of the Studio Movement.

> In both Europe and America the studio ceramist, as distinguished from the industrial artist and craftsman, personifies a youthful movement in an age-old art. . . . [Unlike a traditional artisan,] the studio ceramist is an artist-intellectual who may be an art director, teacher, or any other person who finds creative stimulation in working in clay. His output is wide in scope, ranging from stoneware cups to gigantic pottery jars, and from wall plaques to sculpture in the full round.[130]

Dauterman also saw a marked variety of influences on the contemporary ceramist:

> One senses that our ceramists have found an expanding field of stimulation in ethnological collections as well as art museums. The sculptures of primitive Africa and the pottery of pre-Columbian America provide resources as fertile for our ceramists as the work of the Oriental potters and our heritage from the Old World.

The exhibition was remarkable not only in its recognition of major shifts occurring in the field but in the fact that it included several generations of both European and American ceramists.[131] The Metropolitan was fortunate to acquire a number of pieces from this show.

In 1948 a textile exhibit was organized by John G. Phillips, Jr., the Museum's Coordinator for Industry, in association with the magazine *American Fabrics*. This was virtually a trade show with about two hundred examples in current production.[132]

Only slightly less didactic was a glass exhibit organized two years later by Hugh J. Smith, Jr.[133] Some four hundred objects represented European and American glass over the last half century, including both functional and sculptural pieces. About a hundred works were drawn from the Museum's collection; the rest were borrowed from manufacturers or collectors.

"Glass 1959," however, was an entirely different matter, with a distinguished jury including Edgar Kaufmann, jr., and Gio Ponti, among others.[134] The show, organized by the Corning Museum of Glass, consisted of three hundred pieces of functional and decorative glass produced since 1955 from twenty-three countries. This was the first of several shows done with Corning that would document the dramatic developments in glass.

The field of contemporary metalwork was addressed in 1949 in a show of handmade silver organized by Vincent D. Andrus in the Department of American Decorative Arts.[135] The exhibit consisted of a wide range of material with historical pieces from the sixteenth century to 1900, twentieth-century European work mostly from the Museum's collection, and contemporary American work. A didactic section by the firm Handy & Harman showed how silver was made.

During the two decades that followed World War II, the Museum's greatest commitment — in exhibitions, at least — was to contemporary crafts. After Bach's departure in 1952, however, no individual with a clear vision was left to shape the Museum's role. It would not be until the 1970s that the Metropolitan would return to the field in terms of significant acquisitions.

It was at this time that architecture became a new area of interest for the Museum. These exhibitions were, for the most part, a mixed bag. "American Industry at War" in 1943 included charcoal drawings of dams and factories by the noted renderer Hugh Ferriss.[136] Three years later, the Museum hosted "Houses USA, 1607–1946," a pictorial survey organized by *Life* magazine for the Department of State to circulate in South America.[137] In 1956 the Museum mounted an educational exhibit about the evolution of the public school in New York City from 1806; the show included a section on contemporary schools under construction, featuring architectural renderings and models.[138] Six years later, the Metropolitan used an architectural exhibit as a means to inform the public of its plans to expand the Museum into Central Park.[139] On the occasion of the World's Fair in New York in 1964, the Print Department organized a small exhibit of prints and photographs depicting international expositions from 1851 to 1939.[140] These were all relatively modest exhibitions, but they managed to move the Metropolitan into architecture, an aspect of modern design that had been ignored up to this point, except for its extraordinary installations of European and American period rooms.

The remarkable exception in this series was "Form Givers at Mid-Century," organized in 1959 by Cranston Jones at *Time* magazine and installed by the multitalented designer Gyorgy Kepes.[141] This was the first important exhibition of contemporary architecture to be held at the Metropolitan Museum. It offered an overview of twentieth-century architecture focusing on thirteen noted designers ranging from Frank Lloyd Wright to Eero Saarinen. The exhibit consisted of models, architectural fragments, and photographs by major architectural photographers of this century.

30. "The Arts of Denmark," 1960

The Department of Renaissance and Modern Art also organized four exhibitions of note during this period. In 1946 the Museum showed works of modern Swedish and Danish applied arts in the collection, supplemented by a number of loans.[142] The next year an exhibit of French tapestries featured about sixty modern pieces, including works by Raoul Dufy, Jean Lurçat, and Henri Matisse.[143]

"The Arts of Denmark" (figure 30) — held thirteen years later, in 1960 — was the most important Scandinavian show to be held at the Museum since the Swedish exhibit of 1927.[144] It may also be seen as a harbinger of the Museum's renewed interest in contemporary design. The show was designed by Finn Juhl, the noted Danish architect, and presented the applied arts in a visually exciting installation.[145] Most important, the Metropolitan acquired from the show about two dozen pieces that now constitute the core of its post-World War II Nordic holdings. The pieces were chosen by Edgar Kaufmann, jr., — now departed from MoMA — working with the Metropolitan's curators; this was to be the first of a number of significant collaborations between Kaufmann and the Museum over the next two decades.[146] The response to the Danish exhibition was such that the press noted, "Mr. Rorimer is planning eventually to bring the modern pieces out of hiding and place them on permanent display. He hopes, in the near future, to reinstall the alcoves of modern and Victorian furniture that were eliminated to make space for such additions as the restaurant."[147]

A Russian show mounted two years later could hardly have been more antithetical in subject: 151 objects by the fin-de-siècle goldsmith Carl Fabergé.[148] This was one of the first modern exhibitions of Eastern European design to be held at the Metropolitan, although a number of loan shows with the Soviet Union would follow shortly.

James Rorimer did not live to fulfill his vision of putting the Museum's nineteenth- and twentieth-century decorative arts collections back on view. In 1967 the Trustees picked another young and mercurial director. In his brief decade, Thomas P. F. Hoving radically altered the Metropolitan and changed the public perception of American museums. The creation of a new department for twentieth-century art was among his first acts.

1967–1990

The Metropolitan Museum of Art could hardly have chosen a more opportune moment for returning to the applied arts field, with the enormous changes that were taking place in the mid-1960s with the evolution of the Studio Movement and of the Post-Modernist style. By creating a single department for twentieth-century art, the Museum set an important precedent for the equality of the applied and fine arts, at least in theory, at a time when boundaries were rapidly dissolving and artists were experimenting with multiple disciplines. Objects could now be collected as works of art without being categorized as sculpture or glass or textile. In reality, however, this theory was only partly realized. More than twelve years passed before a full-time curator was hired to coordinate the decorative arts collection, and the applied and fine arts were rarely shown together, either in the permanent galleries or in exhibitions. The department has been in evolution now for almost a quarter of a century, and its history has been shaped in large part by three chairmen and two curators.

The Department of Contemporary Arts was created in 1967 with Henry Geldzahler as its head.[149] He later wrote:

It became apparent that a new department was needed to collect the art of the twentieth century more systematically. By this time it was an inescapable fact that the modernist movement was in the process of becoming a discrete entity and, as such, a necessary part of any encyclopedic museum.

Since New York during the war had surpassed Paris as a center of artistic ferment, and American and European modernists were influencing each other and competing as members of an international movement, it was no longer appropriate to divide responsibility for recent painting and sculpture among four departments. The inclusion of the decorative arts in the new department also made sense from the standpoint of the new postwar internationalism but had more to do with the need to act quickly if New York was ever to have an impressive collection of art deco furniture and objects. Interest in art deco and other neglected realms of collecting was still in the pioneer stage, but it was clear that once a market developed it would skyrocket.[150]

Clearly, principle and market were deciding factors in the creation of this new department.

One of Geldzahler's first tasks was to find out what the Museum owned in the

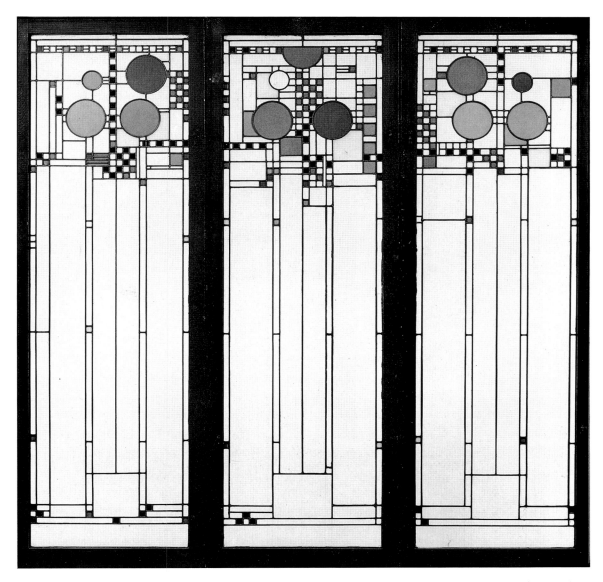

31. Triptych windows designed for the Avery Coonley Playhouse, Riverside, Illinois, in 1912 by Frank Lloyd Wright. Purchase, The Edgar J. Kaufmann Foundation and Edward C. Moore, Jr., Gifts, 1967 (67.231.1–3)

decorative arts and where it was located. The collection was strewn around the building; some of it had even become office furnishings. The new curator realized that one of the most important ways to give the new department visibility was to make acquisitions. During his first year Geldzahler acquired a number of American objects, including the finest stained-glass windows designed by Frank Lloyd Wright (figure 31). He noted, "Gifts such as these move us closer to the dream of this young department: days filled with offers of gifts and funds to make clear the Metropolitan Museum's commitment to the art of our time."[151]

Acquisitions of applied arts during these formative years were small but consistent. Geldzahler wrote: "A particular interest of the department has been to coordinate and fill out the collections of twentieth-century decorative arts previously spread throughout the Museum."[152] The gaps in the Metropolitan's holdings were many, and early acquisitions were often disparate in nature as the department tried to find a focus.

In the next decade the department found its direction. It received a new name in 1970, reflecting its expanded mandate in the field.

The new department's first name, Contemporary Arts, was unsatisfactory; contemporary sounded temporary and arts is one of those words, like moneys, that is diminished in the plural. Modern Art sounded too much like a historical period, and anyway had been pre-empted by another great museum. Twentieth Century Art was the name finally chosen; it encompassed the necessary disciplines and could be effective for several decades as the Museum's collection was brought into the continuing present. Twentieth Century Art is, of course, a temporary designation. While there will always be a certain amount of interest in how this Museum dealt with the art of its own time in the first full century of its existence, it seems clear that eventually the painting, sculpture, and decorative arts of our time will be set in a larger perspective with the past, with the best that has been done. And that is as it should be.[153]

It was also in 1970 that the department found its focus in the applied arts, one that would last for the next sixteen years. Acquisitions would consist primarily of decorative arts from the pre–World War II period and of crafts after the war. In the early 1970s the department began to acquire a wide range of French Art Déco designs from dealers and auctions,[154] and by 1972 a gallery had been reopened for the twentieth-century decorative arts collection. Most important, it was at about this time that Penelope Hunter-Stiebel began a collaboration with Geldzahler as the consultant for the collection, one that would last until 1983.[155] In 1972 she published an important article on the Museum's Art Déco holdings in the *Bulletin*, and this helped to rekindle an interest in the Museum's long involvement with Modern design.[156]

The seventies was thus a decade of vigor and growth for the department. In 1973 an important collection of textiles by Dorothy Liebes was donated, the first of several major textile archives to come to the Museum. In the same year the department purchased three great examples of Art Déco furniture by Jacques Émile Ruhlmann. In 1974 Hunter-Stiebel began to broaden the prewar collection to include other examples of European and American decorative arts in a variety of styles: Arts and Crafts, Art Nouveau, and moderne. Two years later Russel Wright gave the Metropolitan a large selection of his moderne and organic designs, the first large bequest from a living designer. In the mid-1970s the department began to acquire a broad range of contemporary craft — furniture, ceramics, glass, jewelry, and textiles; the latter, in particular, would become a strength of the collection in the 1980s. Through Hunter-Stiebel's perseverance, the Metropolitan was among the first major American museums to make a commitment to the Studio Movement.[157]

In 1977 Geldzahler resigned, but during the same period other important acquisitions of modern design were being made at the Museum. The Department of American Decorative Arts had become particularly active, with its purview now extended to World War I.[158] Three curators helped to shape the late-nineteenth- and early-twentieth-century collections there.

Berry Tracy — one of the great connoisseurs of his generation — came to the

32. "The Rise of an American Architecture," 1970

Museum in 1964 and immediately began making acquisitions eclectically across the board. With the gift of the Kaufmann Fund in 1968–69 and in light of the preparations for the centennial of the Museum in 1970, Tracy quickly assembled a remarkably important collection of American Victorian and Edwardian design, shown for the first time in the exhibition "19th-Century America."[159] Also for the centennial Kaufmann organized the Museum's first scholarly exhibit of modern architecture: "The Rise of an American Architecture, 1815–1915" (figure 32), which was designed by James Stewart Polshek and Arnold Saks.[160]

Tracy had been assisted in the preparation for "19th-Century America" by Marilynn Johnson (Bordes), who joined the Museum at that time as the assistant curator for nineteenth-century American decorative arts.[161] Johnson had an equally fine eye but a greater historical perspective in shaping the collection. She especially extended the Metropolitan's holdings in turn-of-the-century design — both Art Nouveau and Arts and Crafts — but one of her most significant accomplishments was the formation of a "patent" furniture collection: these innovative works of wire, tubular metal, and molded plywood, among other materials, were the precursors for much Modernist design soon to be acquired by the Department of Twentieth Century Art.

In 1978 R. Craig Miller also joined the Department of American Decorative Arts, and when Johnson resigned in 1981, he was placed in charge of the post-1876 decorative

33. Living room designed for the Francis W. Little Residence in 1912–14 by Frank Lloyd Wright.
Purchase, Emily Crane Chadbourne Bequest, 1972

arts collection.[162] He extended the Arts and Crafts holdings with material from the Midwest and the West Coast, and he also formed the Frank Lloyd Wright collection. In 1982 this work was shown in an exhibition that coincided with the opening of the Frank Lloyd Wright room (figure 33).[163] The Department of American Decorative Arts, in collaboration with Twentieth Century Art, also began in the early 1980s to acquire American examples of Art Déco, moderne, and Modernist designs for the Museum; these acquisitions were made possible in large part by the Gamble Fund. In 1984 The American Wing mounted an exhibit of related material: "Design in America: The Cranbrook Vision, 1925–1950," the first large-scale show at the Metropolitan to examine twentieth-century design in an historical context (figure 34).[164]

Two other curators in the Department of American Decorative Arts have expanded the modern holdings there. Frances Gruber Safford has added to the silver collection, while Alice Cooney Frelinghuysen has made extensive acquisitions of glass and ceramics.

The Department of European Sculpture and Decorative Arts has been less active in the period since its mandate extends only to 1900. However, in the last quarter century the Museum has mounted a wide variety of exhibitions including Modern design. Three have been devoted to architecture. An exhibit in 1969 featured the new housing complex envisioned for Welfare (Roosevelt) Island in New York City, and thirteen years later the Museum hosted a drawings show on Rhode Island architecture.[165] Of special note was a

34. Installation shot of "Design in America: The Cranbrook Vision," 1983

retrospective in 1972–73 of the work of Marcel Breuer; organized by Arthur Rosenblatt, the exhibit was the Museum's first one-man show of a living architect.[166] Two other exhibitions were devoted to American Arts and Crafts designers: Will Bradley (1972) and Marie Zimmermann (1985).[167] In 1972 the Metropolitan hosted a show of Eastern European crafts, which included both ancient and contemporary work from the Soviet Union. Similar in nature were two one-material shows devoted to gold (1973) and glass (1983).[168] Finally, a small exhibit of book-bindings by the painter Helen Frankenthaler was shown in 1973.[169] Thus, since 1967 various departments at the Metropolitan have mounted a considerable number of exhibitions devoted to or including Modern design; the Department of Twentieth Century Art itself, however, has not organized any major design shows since its founding — a marked contrast to the prewar records of Joseph Breck and Richard Bach.

In 1979 both the Museum and the Twentieth Century Art department entered a new phase with the appointment of Philippe de Montebello as Director. Thomas Hess served briefly as Consultative Chairman of Twentieth Century Art that year;[170] Penelope Hunter-Stiebel continued as a curatorial consultant and augmented the collection in the areas of prewar decorative arts and contemporary crafts. In 1978 a new installation of the permanent collection featured the Art Déco wall panels for the ocean liner *Normandie* (figure 35). The following year Hunter-Stiebel produced the first comprehensive

35. Glass mural from the Grand Salon of the liner *Normandie*, 1934, by Jean Dupas. Gift of Dr. and Mrs. Irwin R. Berman, 1976 (1976.414.3)

36. The Twentieth Century Design and Architecture Gallery in the Lila Acheson Wallace Wing, photographed in 1987

monograph on the modern decorative arts collection in an issue of the *Bulletin* (Winter 1979/80).

Two decisions for which Philippe de Montebello will be remembered in the field of modern art were the appointment of William S. Lieberman as Chairman in 1979 and the commitment shortly thereafter to build a new wing for twentieth-century art.[171] In that year Hunter-Stiebel was named Associate Curator, the first full-time appointment in the department for the applied arts collection. In 1980 she installed an important exhibition of contemporary craft, "New Glass, A Worldwide Survey," organized by the Corning Museum of Glass.[172] During the next three years she also began to acquire decorative arts from the postwar period. It was finally in 1981 that the many hundreds of American and European objects around the Museum were transferred — technically and physically — to Twentieth Century Art.

In 1983 Craig Miller took over responsibility for the twentieth-century design holdings. A major reevaluation of the collection was begun, resulting in the first substantive conceptual changes since Breck began acquiring objects in 1922. William Lieberman had been a protégé of Alfred Barr for many years at the Museum of Modern Art; he banished the term "decorative arts" and henceforth the Metropolitan's collection would be called "design and architecture." Three areas of the applied arts were to be acquired — the traditional realms of decorative arts and crafts but now also industrial design.[173] The Metropolitan's approach would be comprehensive: acquisitions would be highly selective but across the board, for the Museum would not focus on any one stylistic movement. Moreover, the basis for acquisitions would be an aesthetic one, with sociological, technical, and cultural aspects of secondary importance. In keeping with this approach, objects were generally to be shown as isolated works of art; the department would not install period rooms or re-create ensembles. Following the Museum's general collections policy, the department's emphasis would be on originals, not reproductions, especially mass-produced objects made after an artist's death.[174] The department also began to develop a strict conservation policy of minimal work on objects; since many of the acquisitions were of recent vintage, the goal was to form a collection with original finishes as documents of the evolution of twentieth-century design.

The activities of the design and architecture collection have been somewhat limited over the last seven years, owing to the construction of the new wing. Four installations of the permanent collection (figure 36) were completed during this period to display different aspects of the holdings, as well as new acquisitions (see Appendix A). In 1988 the department collaborated with the Prints department in a small exhibition of architectural drawings collected over the last decade. Also, in May 1987, the department held an international symposium, "20th Century Design and Architecture: Defining a New Tradition." This conference was part of a broad rethinking of the century that was under way at the Museum.[175] This book is itself an outgrowth of that conference, where new ways of looking at the Modern Movement were suggested. It is, in fact, the first catalogue to be published by the Metropolitan on its twentieth-century design holdings.

The most important work in recent years, however, has clearly been in expanding the collection. The department has made hundreds of acquisitions through the assistance of artists, collectors, manufacturers, and dealers. The Hazen/Polsky and Wolf families have been especially supportive. Certainly a major focus has been the formation of an industrial design collection, largely of Modernist works. The department has continued to augment its holdings of pre-World War II decorative arts. Contemporary crafts also continue to be acquired but with a greater emphasis on foreign work; textiles have been an area of special interest, owing to the assistance of Amelia Peck in American Decorative Arts.[176] During this period Twentieth Century Art acquired a number of textile archives, most notably of the Wiener Werkstätte and the Bauhaus. The greatest number of acquisitions, however, have been from the postwar period, as the design collection has been extended up to the present to balance the painting and sculpture holdings. Two areas are of particular interest: late Modernist work, primarily from Italy and Japan, and Post-Modernist material. The latter is perhaps the first such collection assembled by an American museum. The department has also worked in conjunction with Colta Ives and David Kiehl of the Department of Prints and Photographs in acquiring a wide range of decorative and architectural drawings.

Twentieth-century design and architecture holdings at the Metropolitan Museum now number in the thousands, constituting what may be the most comprehensive collection in the Western Hemisphere. This is not to say that there are not significant gaps, for there is much work still to be done. But over the last century the curatorial and educational staff have realized a vision of the Museum's ongoing role in the field. This would certainly not have been possible without the Trustees' original charter and the active support of the administration, but it would have been inconceivable without the artists and patrons who have nourished this Museum. As The Metropolitan Museum of Art prepares to enter a new century, it has forged a remarkable record of achievement and an encompassing mandate for the future.

1890

1920

The Arts and Crafts Movement was a major force in Western design for nearly seven decades. Although it originated in Great Britain during the 1850s, its influence spread within a quarter of a century to Europe and the United States, where it exerted considerable influence until the First World War. Members of the movement shared a philosophy more than a common style, for they were inspired by many different modes deriving from sources as diverse as nature, the Middle Ages, Japonaiserie, and Queen Anne. The leading proponents were John Ruskin and William Morris, who reacted against what they viewed as the catastrophic effects of industrialization and urbanization on the applied arts and, ultimately, on society. They advocated a new design philosophy whose utopian ideals were often in conflict with everyday reality. Nonetheless, many of their precepts have prevailed throughout much of the twentieth century.

One of the fundamental goals of the movement was the elevation of the applied arts to the level of the fine arts: the artisan as artist. Arts and Crafts advocates sought to improve the standard of design for utilitarian objects and to make them readily accessible to the public. They believed that art could improve one's life — both in its creation and in its use. Handcraftsmanship was their weapon against the dehumanizing aspects of

Charles Rohlfs, American.
Clock, ca. 1900

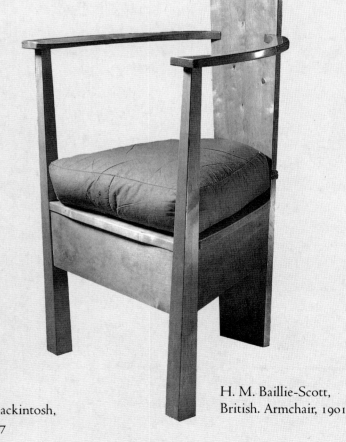

Charles Rennie Mackintosh,
British. Table, 1897

H. M. Baillie-Scott,
British. Armchair, 1901

industrialization; the machine was not, in fact, viewed as a positive factor in design until after 1900. In other ways, however, proponents of the Arts and Crafts Movement were remarkably prescient in advocating the unity of the arts: an egalitarian collaboration of architects and designers, sculptors and painters, as well as a commitment to the total design of one's environment.

Arts and Crafts objects tend to feature simple, solid masses with clearly delineated parts. Designers most often chose tactile materials such as oak, copper, brass, wool, linen, leather, and, occasionally, semiprecious stones. The palette consisted of rich, muted colors: brown, green, ocher, yellow, and russet. Like their fellow Victorians, Arts and Crafts designers often employed stylized motifs derived from nature, but such ornament was now two-dimensional and treated as an intrinsic element in the design rather than as embellishment.

The Arts and Crafts Movement went far beyond matters of style, for its advocates sought a fundamental reorganization of society based on socialist principles. Paradoxically, their sense of form remained rooted in the nineteenth century, but their visionary ideals laid the groundwork for a new century.

Archibald Knox, British.
Spoon, 1902

William de Morgan, British.
Charger, 1898–1917

Dirk van Erp, American.
Lamp, ca. 1912–15

Anonymous. Clock,
ca. 1890–1905

Leona Nicholson, American.
Mug, ca. 1908

Dard Hunter,
American. Vase, ca. 1906

Robert Jarvie, American.
Candlestick, ca. 1901

ALBERT-LOUIS DAMMOUSE, French, 1848–1926

BOWL, 1900–1910
Pâte de verre
H. 2¼ x Diam. 4¼ in. (6 x 11 cm)
Manufacturer: Sèvres
Purchase, Edward C. Moore, Jr., Gift, 1927
27.192.1

PIERRE ADRIEN DALPAYRAT, French, 1844–1910

VASE, ca. 1905
Glazed stoneware
H. 8½ x Diam. 9⅞ in. (21.6 x 25.1 cm)
Purchase, Edward C. Moore, Jr., Gift, 1926
26.228.16

CHARLES ROBERT ASHBEE, British, 1863–1942

BOWL AND SPOON, 1902–4
Silver and chrysoprase
Bowl: H. 3 x W. 10⅝ x D. 4¼ in. (7.6 x 27 x 10.8 cm)
Spoon: L. 6¼ x W. 1¼ x D. 1 in. (15.9 x 3.2 x 2.5 cm)
Manufacturer: Guild of Handicraft
Purchase, Friends of Twentieth Century Decorative Arts
Gifts, 1979
1979.411.1,2

CHARLES SUMNER GREENE, American, 1868–1957
HENRY MATHER GREENE, American, 1870–1954

CHANDELIER, 1907
Designed for the living room of the R. R. Blacker Residence,
Pasadena, California
Mahogany, leaded glass, and bronze
H. 28½ x Diam. 25½ in. (72.4 x 64.8 cm)
Gift of Mr. and Mrs. Barton C. English, 1986
1986.445

OPPOSITE : Detail of border

CHARLES FRANCIS ANNESLEY VOYSEY,
British, 1857–1941

RUG, ca. 1905
From the Gustav Stickley Residence,
Morris Plains, New Jersey
Wool
L. 18 ft. x W. 9 ft. 4 in. (548.6 x 284.5 cm)
Manufacturer : Alexander Morton & Co.
Gift of Cyril Farny, in memory of his wife,
Phyllis Holt Farny, 1976
1976.389.3

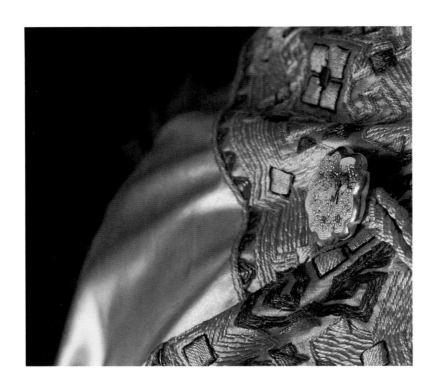

ANONYMOUS, British

DRESS WITH CAPE, ca. 1905
Silk, cotton, metallic thread, and ceramic
Dress: L. (shoulder to floor at front) 60 in. (152.4 cm)
Label: Liberty & Co./London & Paris
Purchase, Friends of the Costume Institute Gifts, 1979
1979.176a–c

ABOVE: Detail of cape clasp

RIGHT: Detail of sleeve

CHARLES RENNIE MACKINTOSH, British, 1868–1928

FOUR ELEVATIONS FOR A LIBRARY, ca. 1894–96
Watercolor and graphite on paper
H. 11⅞ x W. 40 in. (30.2 x 101.3 cm)
Inscribed at bottom: DESIGN FOR A LIBRARY IN A GLASGOW
HOUSE, CHARLES RENNIE MACKINTOSH ARCHITECT,
THIS DRAWING SHEW FOUR SIDES ROOM
Edward Pearce Casey Fund, 1981
1981.189

Details of Mackintosh elevation

WILL H. BRADLEY, American, 1868–1962

PERSPECTIVE OF CHEST, 1901
Designed for *Ladies' Home Journal* (March 1902)
Watercolor, pencil, and ink on paper
H. 8⅝ x W. 4 in. (21.9 x 10.2 cm)
Signed (lower right): W. B.
Gift of Fern Bradley Dufner, 1952
52.625.94

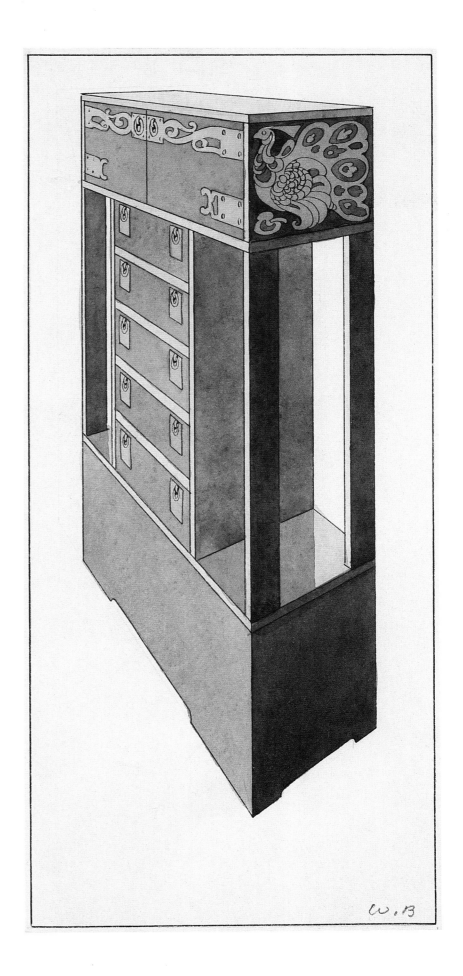

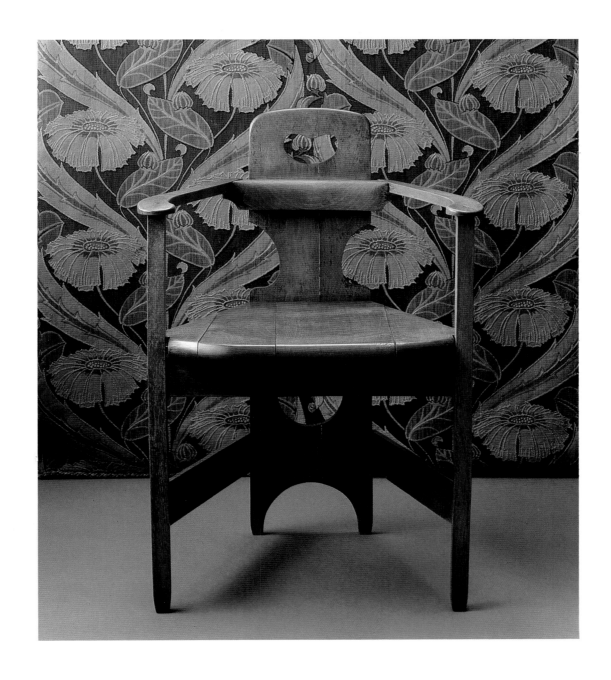

RICHARD RIEMERSCHMID, German, 1868–1957

ARMCHAIR, ca. 1900
Stained beech
H. 32⅜ x W. 22¼ x D. 20¾ in. (82.2 x 56.5 x 52.7 cm)
Manufacturer: J. Fleishchauers Sohne
Purchase, Peter Palumbo Gift, 1987
1987.29

GUSTAV STICKLEY, American, 1857–1942

LIBRARY TABLE, ca. 1905
From the Gustav Stickley Residence, Morris Plains,
New Jersey
Oak, leather, and brass
H. 30 x Diam. 55 in. (76.2 x 139.7 cm)
Gift of Cyril Farny, in memory of his wife,
Phyllis Holt Farny, 1976
1976.389.1

Gustav Gaudernack,
Norwegian. Cup, 1901

More than any style, Art Nouveau captured the essence of the fin-de-siècle. It was recognizable as a European movement by the early 1890s but began to fall into disfavor by the middle of the next decade. Immensely popular on the Continent, Art Nouveau swept through all the arts, but it did not attract a truly serious audience in either England or the United States, nor did it really evolve into a fully integrated architectural style. Art Nouveau was, however, remarkably influential as a decorative mode and may be considered the first original expression of the new century, in that it broke decisively with the succession of nineteenth-century historical revivals and established a new formalist basis for the applied arts.

There were two distinctive aspects to Art Nouveau. One was an exuberant manner with strong ties to the earlier Rococo and Auricular styles, exemplified in France by the sensuous, naturalistic work of Émile Gallé and the École de Nancy. The other was a more restrained, linear mode — typified by the attenuated designs of Henry van de Velde and the mature work of Charles Rennie Mackintosh — which treated the structural frame

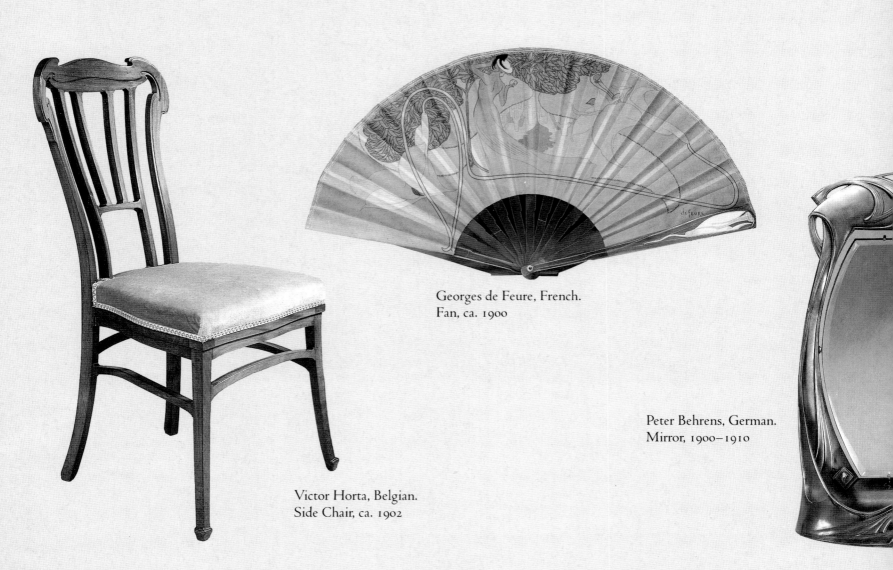

Georges de Feure, French.
Fan, ca. 1900

Victor Horta, Belgian.
Side Chair, ca. 1902

Peter Behrens, German.
Mirror, 1900–1910

as a major element in objects. This idea was to be of the greatest importance for architectonic designers in the twentieth century.

At its best, Art Nouveau is characterized by curvilinear forms in which elements are fused together in a flowing profile, often decorated with rich but shallow relief. The sense of mass varied from taut to pliant; extreme designs affected a deliberate asymmetry and sensuality. The color palette consisted of subdued pinks, lavenders, creams, and greens. Favorite motifs included overwrought stylizations of foliage and insects. Materials were diverse, ranging from silk, velvet, and fruitwood to semiprecious stones and base metals. One of Art Nouveau's greatest triumphs was the transformation of two antithetical industrial materials — cast iron and glass — into ethereal, naturalistic compositions; the designs of Hector Guimard and Victor Horta are among the finest examples.

Art Nouveau was one of the first modes of the new century to appeal to a popular audience, but it was very quickly debased by mass-produced examples that lacked fine craftsmanship. This in no way lessens its importance, however, for Art Nouveau stands as a coda to the eclectic nineteenth century and a prelude to the disjointed century to come.

Émile Gallé, French. "Autumn Crocus" Vase, ca. 1900

Georges de Feure. Vase, 1898–1904

Pierre Adrien Dalpayrat, French, and Louis Comfort Tiffany, American. Lamp, ca. 1900–1901

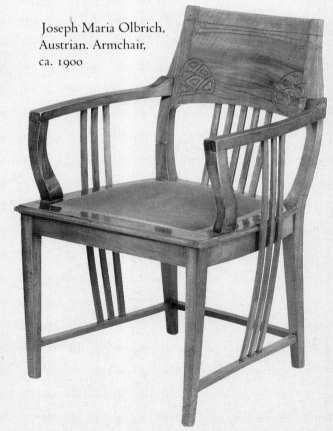

Joseph Maria Olbrich, Austrian. Armchair, ca. 1900

René Lalique, French, 1860–1945

"Coupe Haute Vigne" Cup, 1912
Enameled glass
H. 7 x Diam. 4 in. (17.8 x 10.2 cm)
Manufacturer: René Lalique
Purchase, Edward C. Moore, Jr., Gift, 1923
23.173.1

Teapot and detail of lid

LÉON KANN, French, active at Sèvres 1896–98, 1900–1908

COFFEE SERVICE, 1900–1904
Hard-paste porcelain
Manufacturer: Sèvres
Coffee pot: H. 7 x W. 7⅛ in. (17.8 x 18.1 cm)
Gift of Diane R. Wolf, 1988
1988.287.1–7

ALBIN MÜLLER, German, 1871–1941

TUREEN, ca. 1902
Pewter
H. 14½ x W. 17 x D. 10¼ in. (36.8 x 43.2 x 26 cm)
Manufacturer: Attributed to E. Hueck
Gift of Cynthia Hazen Polsky, 1988
1988.388.5ab

LOUIS COMFORT TIFFANY, American, 1848–1933

LAMP, 1904–15
Bronze and leaded glass
H. 26½ x Diam. 18½ in. (67.3 x 47 cm)
Manufacturer: Tiffany Studios
Gift of Hugh J. Grant, 1974
1974.214.15ab

HECTOR GUIMARD, French, 1867–1942

DRESS PANEL, ca. 1900
Silk and paint
L. 27 x W. 18 in. (68.6 x 45.7 cm)
Gift of Mrs. Hector Guimard, 1949
49.85.11

LEFT: Detail of bodice

BELOW: Detail of train

HOUSE OF WORTH

> DRESS, ca. 1898
> Silk
> Skirt: L. (center back) 42½ in (108 cm)
> Label: Paris/Worth/Paris
> Gift of Eva Drexel Dahlgren, 1976
> 1976.258.1ab

ALPHONSE MUCHA, Czechoslovakian, 1860–1939

DRAWING FOR A FAN, ca. 1899
Watercolor and gold paint on paper
H. 12 x W. 23¼ in. (30.5 x 59.1 cm)
Gift of Janos Scholz, 1963
63.701.1

HENRY VAN DE VELDE, Belgian, 1863–1957

SIDE CHAIR, 1903
Oak and new cotton upholstery
H. 37⅜ x W. 20⅛ x D. 21 in. (94.9 x 51.1 x 53.3 cm)
Manufacturer: H. Schediermantel
Purchase, Lita Annenberg Hazen Charitable Trust Gift, 1985
1985.54.2

GUSTAVE SERRURIER-BOVY, Belgian, 1858–1910

CABINET, 1899
Red narra, ash, glass, copper, and enamel
H. 98 x W. 84 x D. 25 in. (248.9 x 213.4 x 63.5 cm)
Manufacturer: Serrurier
Gift of Mr. and Mrs. Lloyd Macklowe, 1981
1981.512.4

LEFT : Detail of central unit

BELOW : Detail of center drawer

ABOVE: Detail of upper left door

Gerhard Henning, Danish.
Covered Jar, ca. 1920

The rediscovery of the Classical world in the mid-eighteenth century and the formulation of art history as a discipline were cornerstones in the creation of the Modern era. The revival of neoclassical styles that followed — ranging from Adamesque to Biedermeier to Néo-Grec — is thus as much an inherent part of the Modern movement as the preoccupation with industrialization and innovative technology.

After the excitement of the new century began to abate, the perception of Art Nouveau shifted from one of liberation from the past to one of decadence. It is not surprising, then, that designers as widespread as Josef Hoffmann, Eliel Saarinen, Peter Behrens, and Auguste Perret should look to antiquity in their search for order and create a new mode characterized by simple geometric forms with chaste ornament and color. What is unusual, however, is that many of these designers worked in two manners simultaneously: a neoclassical revival for public or domestic commissions and a more functional geometric mode for commercial or institutional projects.

This revivalism exhibited a deliberate diversity as it evolved, and forms often varied from extreme severity to baroque exuberance, especially in Central Europe. Objects were

Patrick Nordstrom,
Danish. Jar, 1917

Josef Hoffmann, Austrian,
born Czechoslovakia.
Bowl, ca. 1920

Adelaide Robineau, American.
"Peruvian Serpent" Bowl, 1917

typically treated as solid masses, but light, planar effects were achieved by a sheathing of elegant veneers or ornamental patterns. The sense of mass could be further negated by stylized fluting, beading, or other types of linear decoration. Designers invariably chose a rich array of materials, including silk, velvet, etched glass, fine woods, and precious metals. Colors were equally strong: intense pink, blue, and red, often placed on a black ground with accents of gold or silver. Stylized figural and floral motifs were used as two-dimensional ornament, often with geometric borders. Such opulence required the finest craftsmanship, although the form of the object itself was rarely an expression of the method of its construction or the materials used.

This historical revival had profound implications for decades to come, for its advocates were the first generation of designers whose careers would extend until mid-century. Even more important, this mode clearly established neoclassicism as the predominant historical tradition for the twentieth century, and nearly every succeeding generation would interpret it in a new guise.

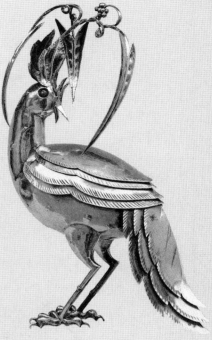

Dagobert Peche, Austrian. Figurine, ca. 1920

Anonymous, Austrian. Four Goblets, ca. 1915–25

Marie Zimmermann, American. Box, ca. 1920

Edward Hald, Swedish, 1883–1980

"Girls Playing with Ball" Bowl and Plate, 1919
Engraved glass
Bowl: H. 9¼ x Diam. 11 in. (23.5 x 27.9 cm)
Plate: H. 1⅛ x Diam. 11⅝ in. (2.9 x 29.5 cm)
Manufacturer: A. B. Orrefors Glasbruk
Gift of Peter M. Brant, 1974
1974.373.1ab

ANDRÉ METTHEY, French, 1871–1920

PLATE, ca. 1910
Earthenware, pâte-de-verre enamel, and gilding
H. 1¾ x Diam. 14⅜ in. (4.4 x 36.5 cm)
Purchase, Edward C. Moore, Jr., Gift, 1924
24.131.5

ABOVE: Detail of spray

DAGOBERT PECHE, Austrian, 1887–1923

JEWEL BOX, ca. 1917
Gilded silver
H. 15⅛ x W. 7¾ x D. 5 in. (38.4 x 19.7 x 12.7 cm)
Manufacturer: Wiener Werkstätte
Purchase, Anonymous Gift, 1978
1978.8a–c

DAGOBERT PECHE, Austrian, 1887–1923

CHANDELIER, 1915–23
Silvered bronze
H. 48½ x Diam. 23⅛ in. (123.2 x 58.7 cm)
Manufacturer: Wiener Werkstätte
Purchase, Edward C. Moore, Jr., Gift, 1923
23.213.1

ABOVE: Detail of ornament

PAUL POIRET, French, 1879–1944

TEXTILE (detail), ca. 1919
Printed silk
H. 70¾ x W. 50¾ in. (179.5 x 129 cm)
Manufacturer: Maison Martine
Purchase, Edward C. Moore, Jr., Gift, 1923
23.14.8

FORTUNY (Mariano Fortuny y Madrazo), Spanish, 1871–1949

DRESS, ca. 1907
Silk, cotton, and glass
L. (shoulder to floor at front) 58 in. (145 cm)
Label: Made in Italy./Fabrique en Italie,/Fortuny, Depose/
Gift of Estate of Agnes Miles Carpenter, 1958
CI 58.61.3ab

Dress twisted for storage in a Fortuny box

Sir Edwin Landseer Lutyens, English, 1869–1944

Elevation and Perspective Studies for
Viceregal Residence, Delhi, ca. 1913–15
Pencil and colored pencil on graph paper
H. 17 x W. 21½ in. (43.2 x 54.4 cm)
Signed (lower left): —of Viceroys Ho/Delhi/original El
Gift of John Harris, 1963
63.681.1

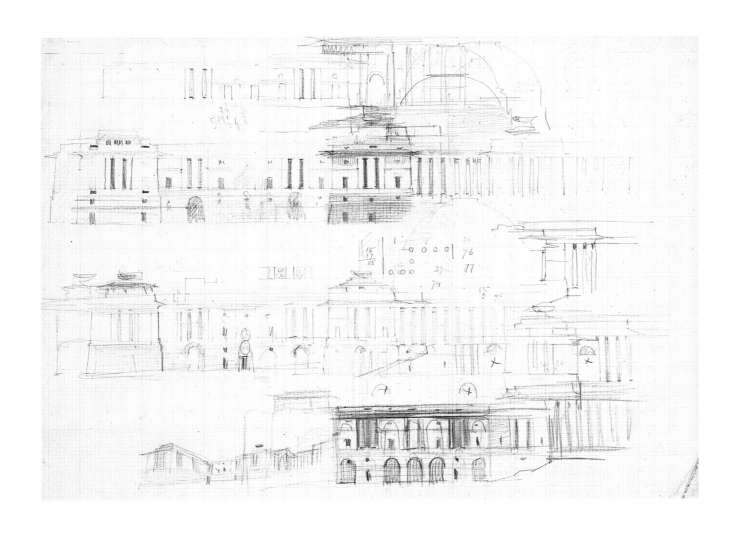

Verso of drawing by Lutyens

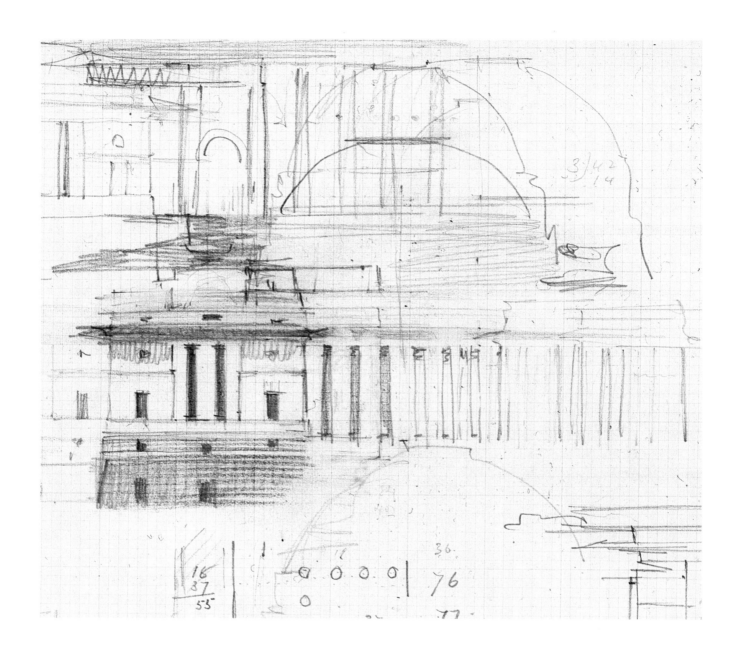

Detail of verso of drawing by Lutyens

BERTOLD LÖFFLER, Austrian, 1874–1960

PERSPECTIVE OF THREE GOBLETS, (detail), ca. 1910
Ink on paper
H. 8⅝ x W. 10⅞ in. (21.8 x 27.7 cm)
Signed (lower left): Bertold Löffler/3 Entwürte für Kelche
Signed (lower right): 700.–
The Elisha Whittelsey Collection, The Elisha Whittelsey
Fund, and Rogers Fund, 1974
1974.509.11

Attributed to JOSEF HOFFMANN, Austrian, born Czechoslovakia, 1870–1956

ARMCHAIR, ca. 1914
Black-stained oak, reproduction cotton upholstery, and new cotton gimp
H. 37¾ x W. 27¼ x D. 21¾ in. (95.9 x 69.2 x 55.2 cm)
Purchase, Lita Annenberg Hazen Charitable Trust Gift, 1986
1987.20

ABOVE: Detail of armrest

RIGHT: Detail of back panel

Jacques Émile Ruhlmann, French, 1879–1933

Desk and Cabinet, ca. 1919
Designed for David David-Weill Residence, Paris
Beech, amboyna veneer, ivory, and shagreen
Desk: H. 37 x W. 47½ x D. 29½ in. (94 x 120.7 x 74.9 cm)
Cabinet: H. 27½ x W. 16½ x D. 28¼ in.
(69.9 x 41.9 x 71.8 cm)
Desk: Purchase, Edgar Kaufmann, Jr., Gift, 1973
1973.154.1
Cabinet: Bequest of Collis P. Huntington, by exchange, 1973
1973.154.3

ABOVE: Detail of drawer pull on desk by Ruhlmann

OPPOSITE: Detail of front of desk

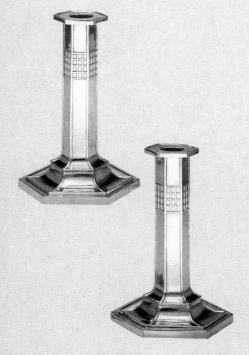

Anonymous, American. Candlesticks, ca. 1901

The art world is not immune to the cyclical swings of fashion, and designers seeking new directions are often attracted to the antitheses of prevailing styles. The search for a new order to supplant Arts and Crafts and Art Nouveau involved not only an historical revival but also, concurrently, a highly reductionist geometric manner.

The genesis of this *neue Sachlichkeit* (new objectivity) was to divest design of the familiar historical and naturalistic motifs used throughout the nineteenth century by a return to basic geometry. One group translated objects into a purist vocabulary of squares, circles, and triangles, an approach that briefly found great favor in Central Europe during the first decade of the century — as with the Wiener Werkstätte (1903–32). A second approach was perhaps more evolutionary, in that it involved the abstraction of natural or figural motifs into geometric patterns. The latter approach was particularly attractive to designers who had evolved out of the Arts and Crafts Movement — such as the American Prairie School. Although it was pervasive and lasted well into the 1910s, its ultimate influence may have been less significant. The very inception of a geometric mode, however, signaled a fundamental rethinking was under way, even if it would not be possible to conceive of a design movement completely without ornament until after World War I. The nineteenth-century tradition of applied decoration had been broken,

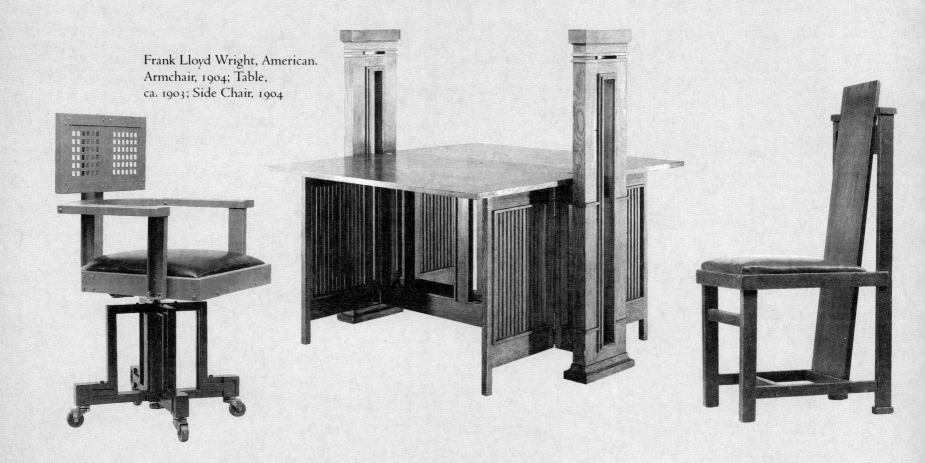

Frank Lloyd Wright, American. Armchair, 1904; Table, ca. 1903; Side Chair, 1904

and henceforth, ornament was to be perceived as an integral part of architectonic design.

Compositions in the geometric mode most often comprised multiples of squares/cubes or circles/cylinders/spheres. Forms tended to be two-dimensional and increasingly horizontal. With less emphasis on mass, the structural frame of an object became more important and was often separately articulated. Negative space in such spare compositions became as important as solid mass, particularly after the introduction of the cantilever. The range of materials, colors, and textures was relatively spartan; Viennese designs in black and white represent the quintessence of the new mode. Most objects were still handmade, although the machine was clearly becoming a major factor in the design process, particularly after Frank Lloyd Wright's pronouncement on "The Art and Craft of the Machine" in 1901. Such new ideas would have far-reaching effects on the design process, for the intellectual concept of an object was increasingly regarded as more important than the traditional demands of construction and utility.

It was not until the 1920s, however, that a second generation of designers — the Modernists — would fully develop these innovative ideas into a machine aesthetic. Half a century later, the geometric mode would emerge again as an important influence on late Modernists seeking to revive pattern and ornament.

Josef Hoffmann, Austrian, born Czechoslovakia. Vase, ca. 1904–6

Francis Jourdain, French. Armchair, ca. 1913

Koloman Moser, Austrian. Cabinet, ca. 1902–4

OTTO PRUTSCHER, Austrian, 1880–1949

STEMWARE, ca. 1905
Enameled glass
H. 8¼ x Diam. 3¼ in. (21 x 8.3 cm)
Manufacturer: Meyrs Neff Glaswerkes
The Cynthia Hazen Polsky Fund, 1989
1989.154

MICHAEL POWOLNY, Austrian, 1871–1954

VASE, ca. 1906
Glazed earthenware
H. 5⅛ x Diam. 3⅛ in. (13 x 7.9 cm)
Purchase, Emilio Ambasz Gift, 1990
1990.97

KARL KIPP, American, active at Roycroft 1908–11, 1915–31

BOWL, ca. 1911
Copper and brass
H. 7⅞ x Diam. 9¼ in. (20 x 23.5 cm)
Manufacturer: Roycroft Copper Shop
Purchase, Theodore R. Gamble, Jr., Gift, in honor of
his mother, Mrs. Theodore Robert Gamble, 1982
1982.118

ARTHUR HEUN, American, 1866–1946

CHANDELIER, ca. 1901–2
Designed for the S. S. Brinsmaid Residence, Des Moines, Iowa
Stained glass and brass
H. 22½ x Diam. 38¾ in. (57.2 x 98.4 cm)
Manufacturer: Giannini and Hilgart Glass Company of Chicago
Gift of Russell L. O'Harra, 1974
1974.357ab

Koloman Moser, Austrian, 1868–1918

"Baummarder" Textile, ca. 1903–7
Printed silk
H. 7 x W. 4⅞ in. (17.8 x 12.4 cm)
Manufacturer: Wiener Werkstätte
Purchase, Rogers Fund, 1954
54.197.6

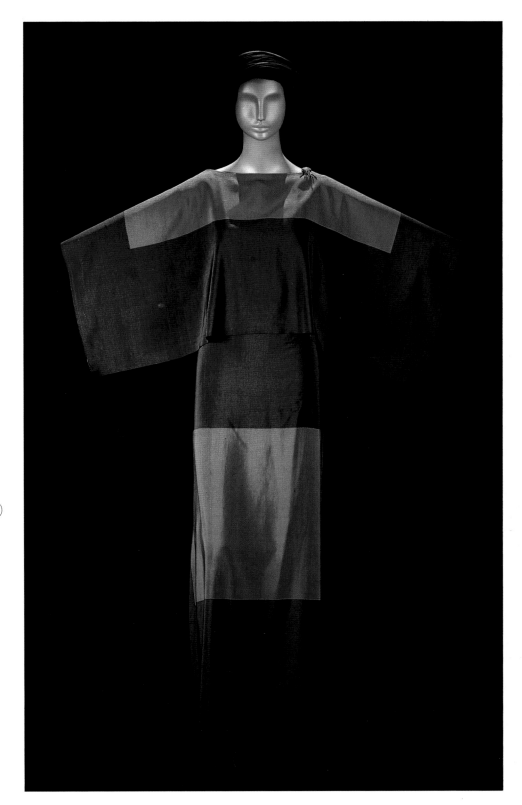

PAUL POIRET, French, 1879–1944

    DRESS AND PONCHO, ca. 1920
    Silk
    Dress: L. (center back) 54 in. (137.2 cm)
    Label: PAUL POIRET/à Paris
    Gift of Mrs. Muriel Draper, 1943
    CI 43.85.2ab

ELIEL SAARINEN, American, born Finland, 1873–1950

PERSPECTIVE OF LIBRARY, 1908
Designed for "Molchow-Haus," the Paul Remer Residence,
near Altruppin, Germany
Ink and pencil on board
H. 10¼ x W. 10¼ in. (26 x 26 cm)
Signed (lower right): ELIEL SAARINEN/A.D. 1908
Promised gift of Mathew Wolf

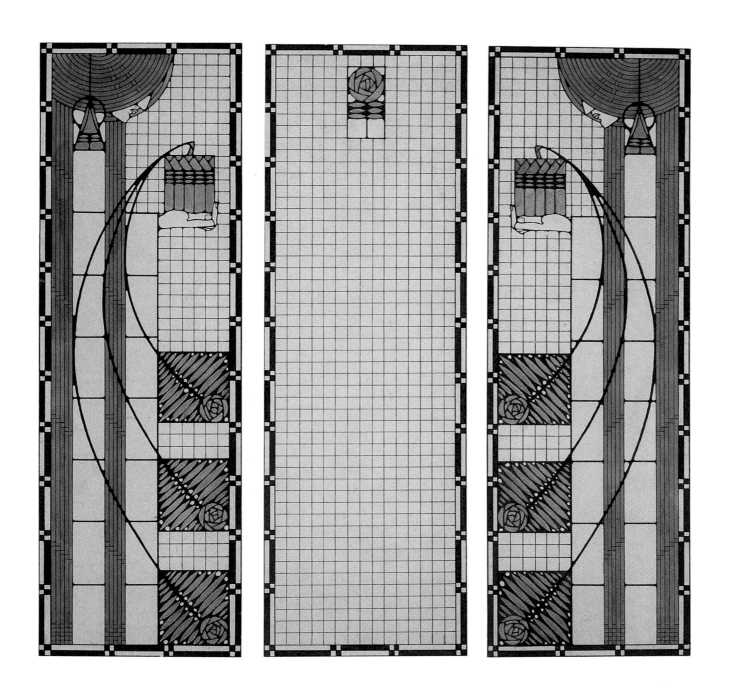

DARD HUNTER, American, 1883–1966

ELEVATION FOR TRIPTYCH WINDOW, ca. 1909
Watercolor and ink on board
Each panel: H. 11⅝ x W. 4 in. (29.5 x 10.2 cm)
Edward Pearce Casey Fund, 1982
1982.1136

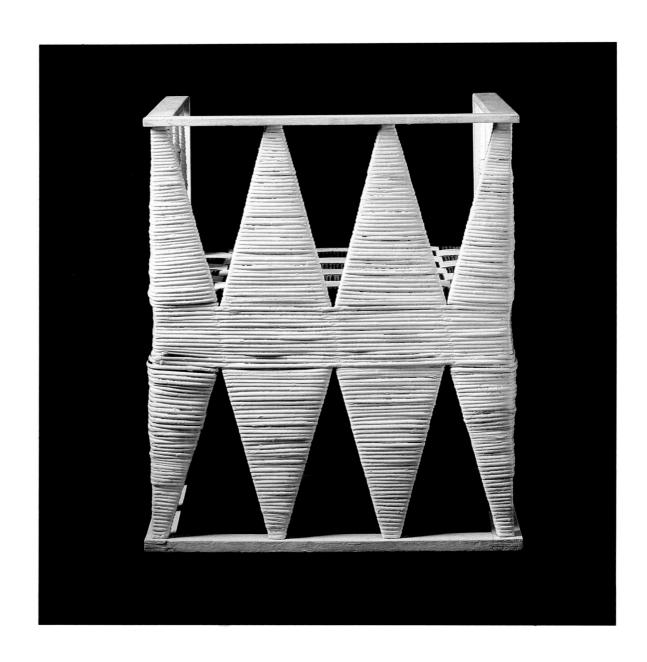

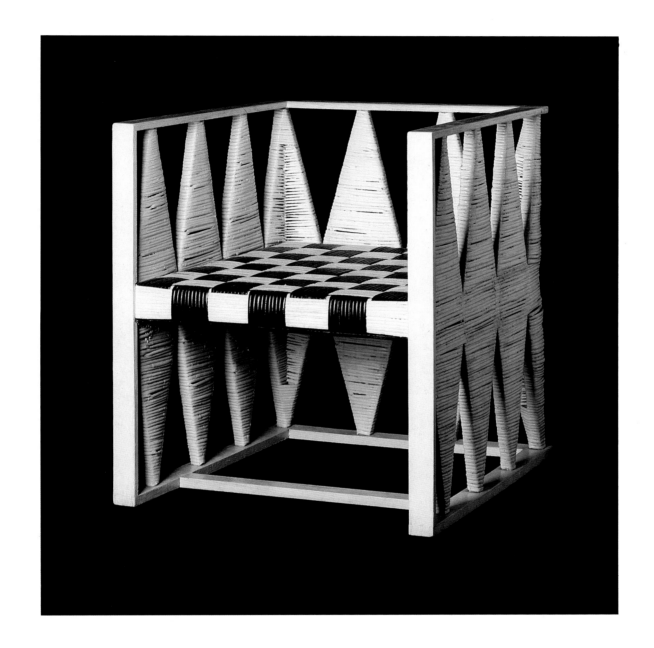

Koloman Moser, Austrian, 1868–1918

Josef Hoffmann, Austrian, born Czechoslovakia, 1870–1956

Armchair, 1903
Designed for Knips Country Residence, Seeboden, Austria
Painted wood and cane
H. 22 x W. 22 x D. 23 in. (55.9 x 55.9 x 58.4 cm)
Manufacturer: Rudnicker
Purchase, Lita Annenberg Hazen Charitable Trust Gift, 1986
1986.146

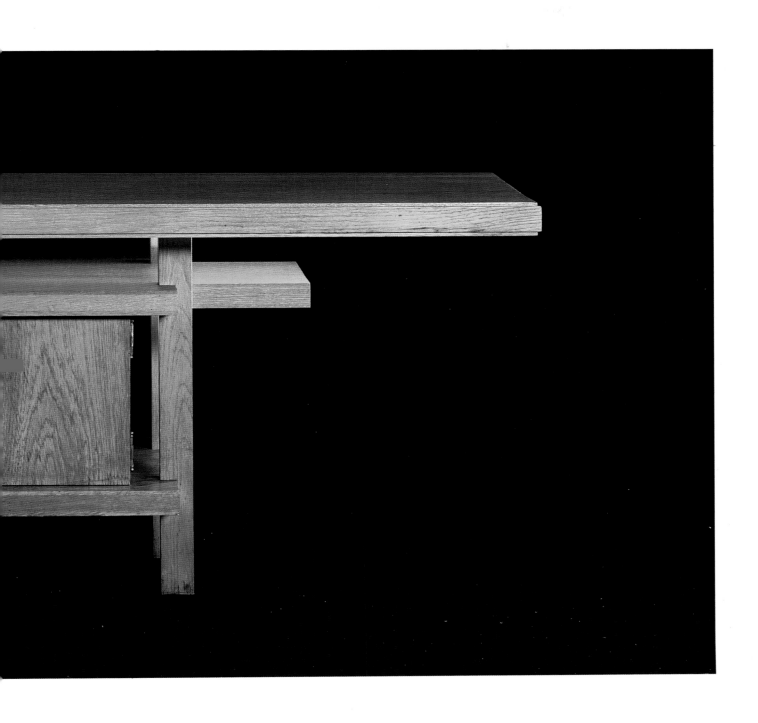

Frank Lloyd Wright, American, 1867–1959

Table, 1912–15
Designed for the Francis W. Little Residence,
Wayzata, Minnesota
White oak
H. 26¼ x W. 72 x D. 27 in. (66.7 x 182.9 x 68.6 cm)
Purchase, Emily Crane Chadbourne Bequest, 1972
1972.69.3

1920

1945

Gerhard Marcks, German.
Coffee Pot, ca. 1930

The First World War demonstrated in a cataclysmic way the overwhelming power of the machine in Western society — for both good and evil. A schism soon developed between those who saw mechanized technology as a means to create a new industrialized society and those who wished to continue the patrician social structure that had existed before the war. In the two decades between the world wars, decorative and industrial designers increasingly pursued divergent courses, creating a breach that would last for nearly half a century. The first generation of designers — including Josef Hoffmann and Peter Behrens, among others — had previously worked in both areas but were soon to find themselves choosing sides. For a second generation the choice was clear-cut. The most revolutionary position was taken by the Modernists, and perhaps no style was to have a more profound or lasting effect on the twentieth century.

The theoretical roots of Modernism may be traced to the Arts and Crafts Movement, although much of its stylistic vocabulary grew out of the more recent geometric mode. Its principal tenets — once radical slogans — have become catchwords: standardization, mass production, and functionalism. Equally important were the belief in a decisive break with historical styles and the conviction that design could change society, which in Europe acquired strong political overtones.

Alfred H. Barr, Jr., the founding director of the Museum of Modern Art, saw as early as 1932, however, that Modernism was above all an aesthetic style. One of its principal proponents, Barr noted in the book *The International Style: Architecture Since 1922* three general characteristics: volumetic space rather than mass, "regularity as opposed to symmetry," and intrinsic rather than applied ornament. The Modernist movement coalesced rapidly after World War I in Europe, and by the late 1920s it had become a major style through the avid proselytizing of its brilliant advocates — historians such as

Marcel Breuer, American,
born Hungary.
"B35" Armchair, 1928–29

Ludwig Mies van der Rohe, American,
born Germany. "Brno" Armchair,
ca. 1930

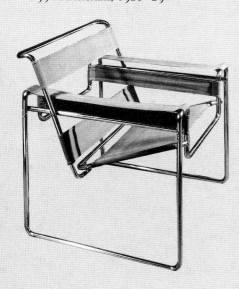

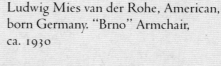

Marcel Breuer. "Club" Armchair, ca. 1925

Nikolaus Pevsner and Siegfried Giedion and organizations such as the Bauhaus (1919–33), CIAM (Congrès Internationaux d'Architecture Moderne, begun 1928), and the Museum of Modern Art (founded 1929). Even more influential, however, were Modernism's principal designers: Marcel Breuer, Walter Gropius, Le Corbusier, and Ludwig Mies van der Rohe.

Consistent with their functionalist outlook, the Modernists believed that form was derived from use, material, and method of production. In actuality, most of their earliest work was handmade, but they clung to the curious aesthetic precept that the use of simple geometric forms could give the appearance of industrial production. Mies's Barcelona chair (1929) remains perhaps the most compelling example of this. Modernist designers tended to employ a minimum of parts in the handling of form, often fusing elements to create a single, strong profile. When parts were articulated, function or material was generally a determining factor. The Modernist palette usually consisted of white and gray accented with black or primary hues. The surface textures of an object could contrast sharply, but any ornamentation had to be integral to the materials or the construction. Designers were eager to use the latest technologies for handling steel, glass, concrete, and, later, laminated wood. The innate qualities of these materials were often exaggerated to achieve effects of resilience, lightness, or transparency.

The ultimate goal of this fascination with industrial technology was to mass-produce objects that were handsome, inexpensive, and easy to care for. This Modernist ideal was to remain the dominant Western design aesthetic until the 1960s. Only then was the debate between industrial and decorative designers renewed and the search for a new order begun.

Aino Aalto, Finnish. Pitcher and Tumblers, ca. 1930

Donald Deskey, American. Tables, ca. 1930

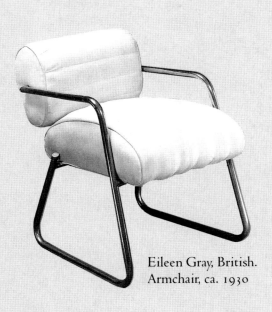

Eileen Gray, British. Armchair, ca. 1930

Gilbert Rohde, American. Armchair, ca. 1930

WILHELM WAGENFELD, German, born 1900

TEA SERVICE, 1930–34
Glass
Teapot: H. 5¾ x W. 9⅝ x D. 5⅞ in. (14.6 x 24.4 x 14.9 cm)
Manufacturer: Jenaer Glas
Gift of Barry J. Friedman and Patricia Pastor, 1983
1983.522.1–23

TRUDE PETRI, German, 1906–68

      "URBINO" DINNERWARE, ca. 1930–34
      Porcelain
      Tureen (center): H. 6 x Diam. 11½ in. (15.2 x 29.2 cm)
      Manufacturer: Staatliche Porzellan-Manufaktur Berlin
      The Cynthia Hazen Polsky Fund, 1989
      1989.203.1ab–5

ANDREAS MORITZ, German, born 1901

SALT AND PEPPER SERVICE, 1929
Silver
Salt dish: H. ¾ x Diam. 2¾ in. (1.9 x 7 cm)
Pepper shaker: H. 1¾ x Diam. 1¼ in. (4.4 x 3.2 cm)
Gift of Andreas Moritz, 1982
1982.51.6–8

EILEEN GRAY, British, 1878–1977

"LANTERNE JAPONAISE" CHANDELIERS, ca. 1935
Painted steel, perspex, and glass
H. 16⅞ x W. 10¾ x D. 10¾ in.
(42.9 x 27.3 x 27.3 cm)
Gift of Seymour Stein, 1984
1984.564.1,2

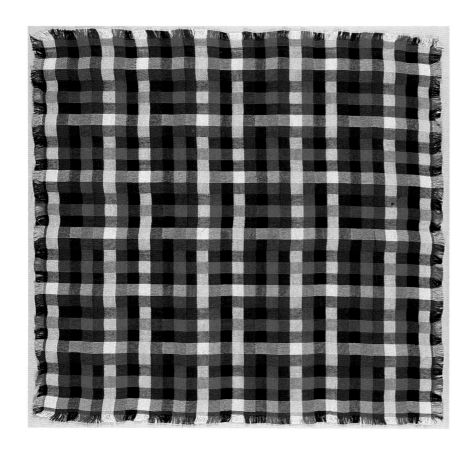

GRETE REICHARDT, German, 1907–84

TEXTILE, ca. 1919–27
Woven cotton and rayon
H. 25¼ x W. 25 in. (64.1 x 63.5 cm)
Gift of Jack Lenor Larsen, 1985
1985.198.61

CLAIRE McCARDELL, American, 1905–58

LOUNGING PAJAMAS, 1938
Rayon, leather, and brass
L. (center back) 57¼ in. (145.4 cm)
Manufacturer: Townley Frocks, Inc.
Gift of Claire McCardell, 1949
CI 49.37.2ab

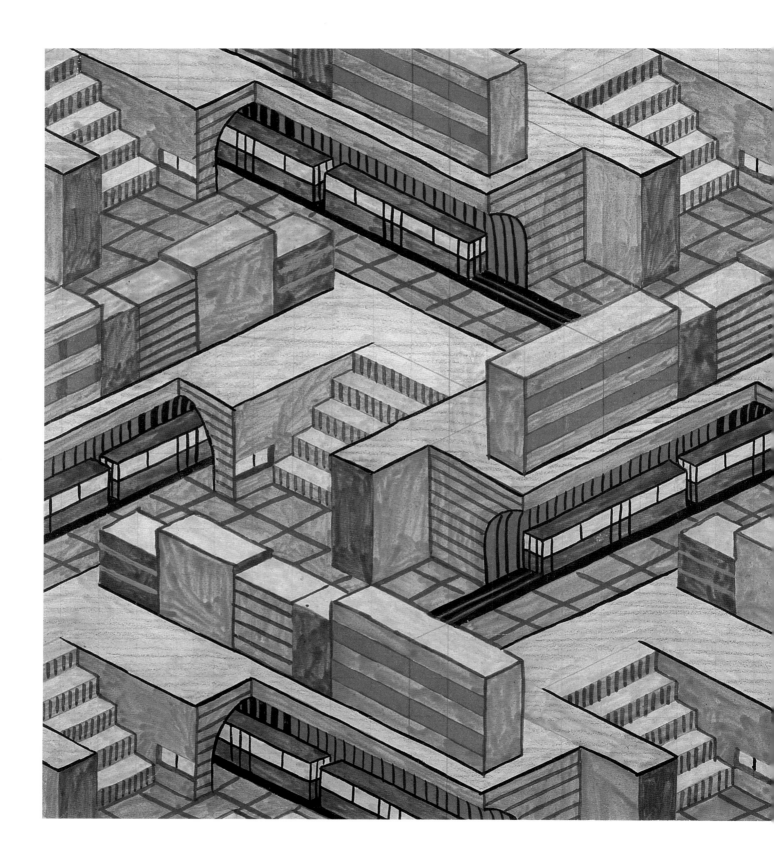

Lena Bergner Meyer, German, 1906–81

Drawing for "Metro" Textile, 1932
Gouache and pencil on paper
H. 8¼ x L. 11¼ in. (21 x 28.6 cm)
Gift of Jack Lenor Larsen, 1985
1985.198.41

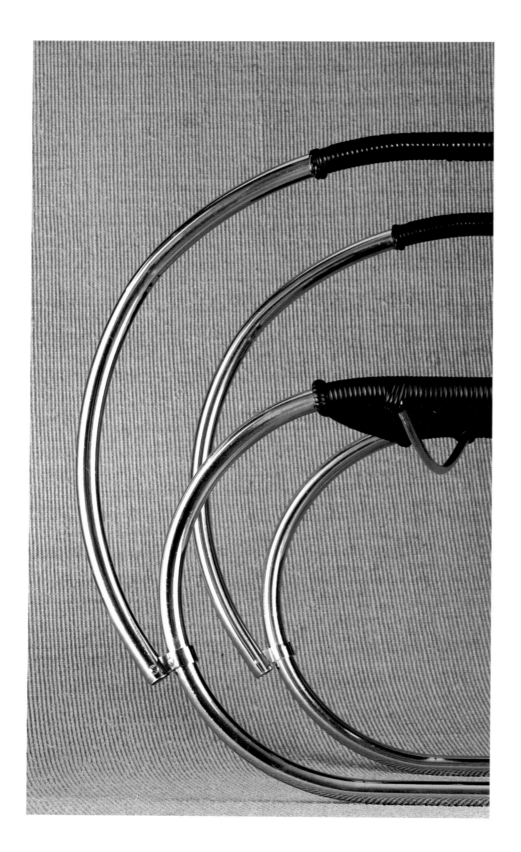

LUDWIG MIES VAN DER ROHE, American, born Germany, 1886–1969

"MR" ARMCHAIR, 1927
Chrome-plated steel and painted cane
H. 31 x W. 20½ x D. 32½ in. (78.7 x 52 x 82.6 cm)
Manufacturer: Berliner Metallgewerbe Joseph Müller
Purchase, Theodore R. Gamble, Jr., Gift, in honor of his
mother, Mrs. Theodore Robert Gamble, 1980
1980.351

CHARLOTTE PERRIAND, French, born 1903

CABINET, ca. 1939
Designed for the Charlotte Perriand Apartment, Paris
Aluminum, painted steel, pine, and walnut
H. 49 x W. 99⅞ x D. 17⅞ in. (124.5 x 253.7 x 45.4 cm)
Gift of Mr. and Mrs. Michael Chow, 1987
1987.461.2ab

Frank Lloyd Wright,
American. Side Chair,
ca. 1937

Modernism had barely been codified in the Museum of Modern Art's landmark show "Modern Architecture: International Exhibition" (1932) before a widespread reaction set in. This multifarious response was not an organized movement constituting a style, but it was certainly a recognizable mode, one usually described as "organic" or "biomorphic." During the 1930s Modernist designers themselves — such as Alvar Aalto and Marcel Breuer — began to explore new directions, particularly in their choice and handling of materials. In the United States, Frank Lloyd Wright returned to prominence in 1936 after years of seeming inactivity, and a young generation of California architects received recognition for their vernacular wooden designs. After the Modernist exhibition of 1929 in Stockholm, Scandinavia also moved to the forefront, and "Swedish Modern" became a household word during the thirties. Of particular significance was the concurrent interest in design shown by Parisian painters and sculptors, especially the Surrealists.

The influence of French artistic circles was ostensibly the least important aspect of this organic mode. However, the precedent set by Joan Miró, Salvador Dali, and Frederick Kiesler with their fascination for nihilism, the subconscious, and the irrational was to have far-reaching consequences in the applied arts of the 1960s, particularly in a new definition of craft. This highly sculptural work also foreshadowed the generation of artist-designers that emerged in the 1970s.

In terms of mainstream design, the reaction to Modernism is more evident, as designers turned from an emphasis on the machine to an interest in man and nature. An

Bruno Mathsson, Swedish.
Armchair and Footrest, ca. 1935

Alvar Aalto, Finnish.
"31" Armchair, 1930–33

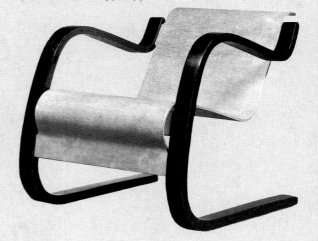

important aesthetic shift occurred in how form was derived. The Modernists accepted geometric form a priori, but other designers, such as Eric Mendelsohn and Frank Lloyd Wright, pursued an alternative approach, in which unique forms were specially generated for projects. This idea would have a significant influence after World War II on a third generation.

Although the organic mode was diverse, there were a number of common characteristics. Hard-edged geometric forms gave way to softer, more irregular shapes, with flowing lines unifying the object's profile. Designers used a mixture of materials for their contrasting textures; in particular, wood — bent and laminated in highly sculptural configurations — replaced steel and glass. Textile designers were drawn to strong weaves and colors. After an absence of any ornamentation, flat patterns returned to favor, and colors changed from primary to muted hues: favorites were dusty rose, chartreuse, dark green, and brown. In terms of construction, materials were used in an expressive manner, for questions of mass production and functionalism had become less central. Designers were now more concerned with the shaping of objects to accommodate the human body, an important antecedent of the field of ergonomics that developed after World War II.

Designers working in the organic manner did not produce a significant body of work, owing to the onset of war. However, they did succeed in modifying the course of Modernism, and, in the second half of the century, this mode would have substantial aftereffects, both stylistically and philosophically.

Viktor Lindstrand, Swedish. Vase, 1939

Joan Miró, Spanish. Vase, 1942

James Prestini, American. Sculpture, 1939–42

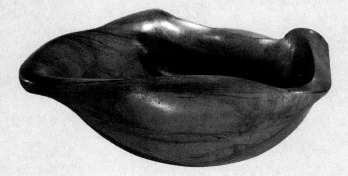

Russel Wright, American. Bowl, ca. 1940

EDVIN OHRSTROM, Swedish, 1883–1980

VASE, 1939
Glass
H. 8$\frac{1}{8}$ x Diam. 7$\frac{1}{4}$ in. (20.6 x 18.4 cm)
Manufacturer: A. B. Orrefors Glasbruk
Purchase, Edward C. Moore, Jr., Gift, 1939
39.154.5

RUSSEL WRIGHT, American, 1904–76

"AMERICAN MODERN" DINNERWARE, 1937
Earthenware
Pitcher (far left): H. 10¾ x Diam. 8¾ in. (27.3 x 22.2 cm)
Manufacturer: Steubenville Pottery
Pitcher: Gift of Jane and Arnold Adlin, 1989
1989.395
Salt shakers, coffee pot: Gift of Laurence B. Kanter, 1990
1990.69.1–3
Celery dish, small pitcher: Gift of Paul F. Walter, 1990
1990.73.1,2

JOHANN ROHDE, Danish, 1856–1935

PITCHER, 1933–37
Silver
H. 9¼ x Diam. 5 in. (23.5 x 12.7 cm)
Manufacturer: Georg Jensen
The Cynthia Hazen Polsky Fund, 1989
1989.258

Dorothy Liebes, American, 1897–1972

Textile, ca. 1934
Silk, Lurex, and cotton
L. 7 x W. 6 in. (17.8 x 15.2 cm)
Gift of Dorothy Liebes Design, Inc., 1973
1973.129.10

Sleeve detail of dress by Adrian (OVERLEAF)

ADRIAN (Gilbert Adrian Greenburgh), American, 1903–59

DRESS AND CAPE, ca. 1945
Rayon
Cape: L. (center back) 65½ in. (166.4 cm)
Label: Adrian/CUSTOM
Gift of Eleanor Lambert, 1958
CI 58.25abc

Eric Mendelsohn, American, born Germany, 1887–1953

Exterior Perspectives of Four Buildings,
ca. 1935
Graphite on tissue paper
H. 11½ x W. 9 in. (29.2 x 22.8 cm)
Signed (lower left): MENDELSOHN
Edward Pearce Casey Fund, 1986
1986.1088

FERNAND LÉGER, French, 1881–1955

ELEVATION OF A MURAL FOR FIREPLACE WALL
(detail), ca. 1939
Pencil, ink, and watercolor on paper
H. 5¼ x W. 17⅜ in. (13.3 x 44.1 cm)
Inscribed (bottom center): l'etoule de mer/et les plongeurs
Gift of Wallace K. Harrison, 1972
1972.730.1

ALVAR AALTO, Finnish, 1898–1976

CHAISE LONGUE, 1936–37
Molded plywood and cotton webbing
H. 28⅞ x W. 24¼ x D. 60 in. (73.3 x 61.6 x 152.4 cm)
Manufacturer: Artek
Purchase, Theodore R. Gamble, Jr., Gift, in honor of his
mother, Mrs. Theodore Robert Gamble, 1985
1985.211

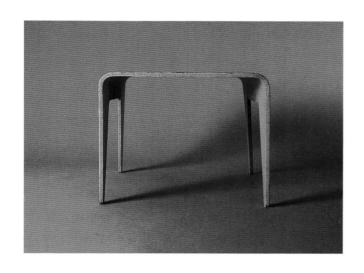

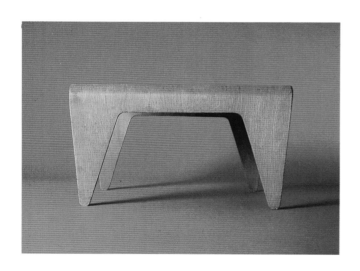

MARCEL BREUER, American, born Hungary, 1902–81

TABLE, 1936
Molded plywood
H. 13⅝ x W. 24 x D. 16½ in. (34.6 x 61 x 41.9 cm)
Manufacturer: Isokon
Gift of Daniel and Suzanne Geller, in memory of
Bert and Phyllis Geller, 1989
1989.52

Maurice Marinot, French.
Covered Vase, ca. 1925

The term Art Déco has been used in recent years to describe almost every facet of the applied arts produced between the world wars. Here its use is restricted to decorative design produced in the decade following World War I. France was the wellspring of Art Déco, and after the Exposition Internationale des Arts Décoratifs et Industriels Modernes was held in Paris in 1925, the style enjoyed enormous popularity elsewhere in Europe and, briefly, in America. It was in many ways a continuation of the historical revivalism that had begun in the first decade, but there were important differences. Art Déco was a far more concerted effort, if not a full-scale movement. Designers worked exclusively in a single manner, rather than several, and increasingly found themselves to be defenders of the old guard against the radical, utopian Modernists.

Art Déco drew on a number of neoclassical sources — from Louis XVI to Louis Philippe. The influence of avant-garde painting and sculpture, particularly the Fauves and the Cubists, has often been noted. Both groups, however, were too radical and intellectual to have had a fundamental impact on such a decorative and revivalistic style, although Art Déco designers often borrowed strong colors, geometric patterns, and even African motifs for their work. This in no way lessens Art Déco's importance in the Modern era; it remains the quintessential statement of decorative design in the twentieth century.

Art Déco objects generally feature a solid mass with a clear delineation of parts.

Clement Rousseau,
French. Table, 1924

Karl Malmsten, Swedish.
Side Chair, ca. 1927

Bruno Paul, German.
Dressing Table and Stool, ca. 1924

The handling of the surface was of paramount importance, and planar forms were often enlivened by gently curving profiles accentuated by shallow carving or fluting. Finishes included rich veneers, lacquer, or gilding. To heighten such surface effects, proportions were sometimes slightly exaggerated or overscaled to achieve a sense of verticality. The consummate master of such subtlety was the French designer Jacques Émile Ruhlmann.

Art Déco designers reveled in a luxurious vocabulary. Favorite materials — including macassar, ebony, amboyna, silk, and bronze — were often further embellished with shagreen, ivory, or gold. Colors were bold and elegant: red or green against black, gold, or silver. Strong pattern and ornament were an essential part of the Art Déco style, and designers frequently used swags, garlands of fruit and flowers, animals, and jets of water as motifs for fabrics and wallpapers. Furniture featured elaborate inlays and ormolu mounts. Such a sumptuous aesthetic required traditional craftsmanship at an extraordinary level. Consequently, Art Déco design often involved the collaboration of a number of artists, whether for a single object or an ensemble.

The Art Déco style was, of course, the reflection of an opulent and leisured world that could not be maintained after the onset of the Depression in 1929. It would be nearly half a century before major designers would again turn their attention to the traditional realm of decorative form and pattern.

Jean Dunand, French, born Switzerland. Vase, 1920–30

Émile Lenoble, French. Vase, ca. 1925

Edward Hald, Swedish. "Fireworks" Vase, 1921

René Lalique, French. "Nadica" Vase, 1936

Georges Bastard, French. Fan, ca. 1925

René Buthaud, French. Vase, 1925

Georg Jensen, Danish. Tureen, ca. 1925

Simon Gate, Swedish, 1883–1945

Vase, 1926
Engraved glass
H. 11⅛ x Diam. 10¾ in. (28.3 x 27.3 cm)
Manufacturer: A. B. Orrefors Glasbruk
Purchase, Edward C. Moore, Jr., Gift, 1927
27.96.1

GIO PONTI, Italian, 1891–1979

URN, 1924
Porcelain
H. 19¾ x Diam. 6⅝ in. (50.2 x 16.8 cm)
Manufacturer: Richard Ginori
Purchase, Edward C. Moore, Jr., Gift, 1931
31.83ab

Sugar bowl, detail of tea and coffee service
by Puiforcat (OVERLEAF)

Jean Puiforcat, French, 1897–1945

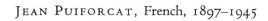
Tea and Coffee Service, ca. 1923
Silver, lapis lazuli, and ivory
Tray: H. 2 x W. 27¾ x D. 23½ in. (5.1 x 70.5 x 59.7 cm)
Purchase, Edward C. Moore, Jr., Gift, 1923 and 1925
23.177.1–3, 25.230.1–4

Detail of teakettle by Puiforcat

Jacques Émile Ruhlmann, French, 1879–1933

Lamp, ca. 1926
Bronze and alabaster
H. 29½ x Diam. 13¾ in. (74.9 x 34.9 cm)
Gift of Mr. and Mrs. Michael Chow, 1985
1985.430.21

ABOVE: Detail of second panel from left

BELOW: Detail of right panel

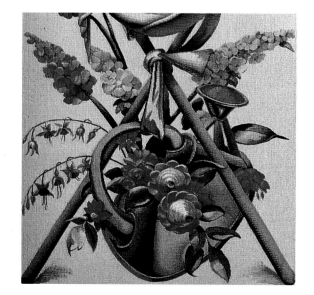

PAUL VÉRA, French, 1882–1958

"THE GARDENS" FOLDING SCREEN, 1923–24
Wool, silk, and mahogany
H. 79 x W. 122 in. (200.7 x 309.9 cm)
Manufacturer: Manufacture Nationale de Beauvais
Frame: designed by Paul Follot, French, 1877–1941
Purchase, Edward C. Moore, Jr., Gift, 1932
32.99

MADELEINE VIONNET, French, 1877–1975

DRESS, 1932
Silk
L. (shoulder to floor at front) 61¾ in. (156.8 cm)
Label: Madeleine Vionnet 92316
Gift of Toni Frissell Bacon, 1974
CI 1974.81.1

Erik Gunnar Asplund, Swedish, 1885–1940

Plan and Elevation for Swedish Pavilion,
Paris Exposition (details), 1924
Ink and gouache on board
H. 13¾ x W. 13¾ in. (34.9 x 34.9 cm)
Signed (lower right): STUDIO/STHLM.28:8:24/E.G.
Asplund
Edward Pearce Casey Fund, 1984
1984.1168.1,2

HUNT DIEDERICH, American, 1884–1953

DRAWING FOR A FIRESCREEN, ca. 1925
(verso and recto)
Crayon and chalk on paper
H. 31⅜ x 23⅞ in. (79.6 x 60.6 cm)
Gift of Frederic Newlin Price, 1955
55.171.15

LOUIS SÜE, French, 1875–1968

ANDRÉ MARE, French, 1887–1932

ARMCHAIR, ca. 1925
Designed for the Musée d'Art Contemporain Pavilion,
Exposition Internationale des Arts Décoratifs et
Industriels Modernes, Paris
Ebony and new leather upholstery
H. 34¼ x W. 24 x D. 19 in. (87 x 61 x 48.3 cm)
Manufacturer: Compagnie des Arts Français
Purchase, Edward C. Moore, Jr., Gift, 1925
25.209.2

LEFT : Detail of cornice

BELOW : Detail of front leg

JACQUES ÉMILE RUHLMANN, French, 1879–1933

CABINET, 1925
Macassar ebony, ivory, and amarant
H. 50¼ x W. 33¼ x D. 17 in. (127.6 x 84.5 x 43.2 cm)
Purchase, Edward C. Moore, Jr., Gift, 1925
25.231.1

Details of center inlay

Gilbert Rohde, American.
Side Chair, ca. 1934

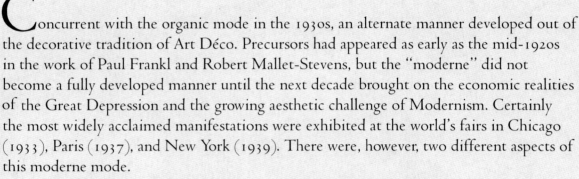

Concurrent with the organic mode in the 1930s, an alternate manner developed out of the decorative tradition of Art Déco. Precursors had appeared as early as the mid-1920s in the work of Paul Frankl and Robert Mallet-Stevens, but the "moderne" did not become a fully developed manner until the next decade brought on the economic realities of the Great Depression and the growing aesthetic challenge of Modernism. Certainly the most widely acclaimed manifestations were exhibited at the world's fairs in Chicago (1933), Paris (1937), and New York (1939). There were, however, two different aspects of this moderne mode.

One expression involved decorative designers who had initially worked in the Art Déco style but who increasingly sought a new direction after the 1925 Exposition. Among the most notable were designers associated with the UAM (Union des Artistes Modernes, founded 1929), who usurped the Modernist vocabulary of form and material but employed it in a decidedly decorative rather than architectonic manner. Such moderne designers could not accept the extreme austerity of the International Style and wished to preserve a sense of mass, ornament, and pattern in work that remained mostly handmade. This stylistic adaptation of Modernism led to the use, at that time, of the pejorative terms "modernistic" and "streamlined."

The second aspect of the moderne involved the emergence of the industrial designer in the United States during the late 1920s and early 1930s. These designers used a similar streamlined vocabulary as their decorative counterparts, but their theoretical

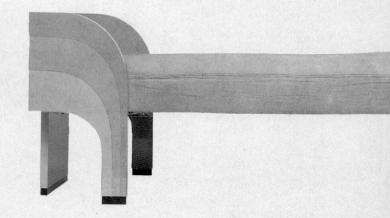

Jean Dunand, French,
born Switzerland.
Table, 1928

Paul Frankl, American,
born Germany. Bookcase,
ca. 1925–30

approach was quite different. Their objects — which really *were* mass-produced — ranged from packaging and appliances to interiors, and even trains. Unlike earlier designers for industry, these new industrial designers were not trained as architects or artists but came most often out of the worlds of advertising, retailing, or theater. Their approach to design was thus not based on a rigorous intellectual concept but simply on the stylization of objects for mass consumption. Ultimately, this would entail a profound shift in the accessibility of modern design, from an avant-garde elite to the middle class, and most importantly, it marked a completely new aesthetic approach to the applied arts.

Such a dramatic shift in design could only occur after fundamental changes had taken place in society. Industrialization, for example, had unleashed a host of forces — the widespread use of electricity, the combustion engine, department-store retailing, assembly-line manufacture, international markets, and consumer advertising, to name only a few. A multitude of new inventions had been generated in the process: cars, airplanes, refrigerators, typewriters, washing machines, radios, telephones, and even cocktail shakers. If these products were to be produced for a mass market, new archetypal forms were needed. The industrial designer's solution in the 1930s was the creation of a universal housing: a planar shell with rounded edges, often accentuated with asymmetrical, horizontal banding, and one with as few parts and joints as possible. Even traditional objects were restyled to this configuration.

Robert Lallemont, French. Vase, 1927

René Lalique, French. Goblets, 1933

Kem Weber, American, born Germany. Clock, ca. 1930

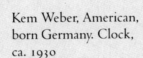

Jean Puiforcat, French. Bowl, 1934

Jules Bouy, American, born France. Chaise Longue, ca. 1930

WALTER DORWIN TEAGUE, American, 1883–1960

EDWIN W. FUERST, American, 1903–88

> "EMBASSY 4900" STEMWARE, 1939
> Glass
> Goblet at right: H. 6½ x Diam. 3¾ in. (16.5 x 9.5 cm)
> Manufacturer: Libbey Glass Company
> Gift of Lillian Nassau, 1981
> 1981.139.1,2

MAIJA GROTELL, American, born Finland, 1899–1973

VASE, 1940
Glazed stoneware
H. 15¾ x Diam. 10¾ in. (40 x 27.3 cm)
Purchase, Edward C. Moore, Jr., Gift, 1940
1940.153.1

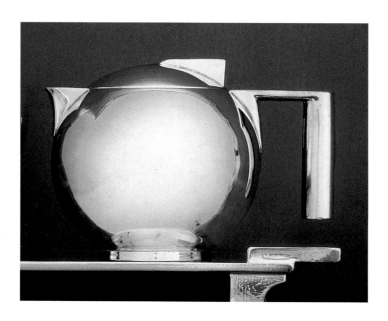

LEFT : Detail of tray and creamer

PAUL LOBEL, American, 1899–1983

TEA SERVICE, 1934
Silverplate and wood
Tray: L. 18 x W. 8⅛ x H. 1 in. (45.7 x 20.6 x 2.5 cm)
Manufacturer: Wilcox Silverplate Company,
Division of International Silver Company
Gift of M. H. Lobel and C. H. Lobel, 1983
1983.493.1–4

Jules Bouy, American, born France, 1872–1937

Lamp, 1930
Copper, brass, and frosted glass
H. 24½ x W. 7¾ x D. 7¾ in. (62.2 x 19.7 x 19.7 cm)
Gift of Juliette B. Castle and Mrs. Paul Dahlstrohm, 1968
68.70.17

ILONKA KARASZ, American, born Hungary, 1896–1981

CARPET, 1928
Designed for a nursery in the American Designers'
Gallery, Inc., Exhibition, New York
Cotton and wool
L. 107½ x W. 107 in. (273.1 x 271.8 cm)
Purchase, Theodore R. Gamble, Jr., in honor of his mother,
Mrs. Theodore Robert Gamble, 1983
1983.228.3

ELSA SCHIAPARELLI, Italian, 1890–1973

COAT, 1939
Silk
L. (center back) 64 in. (162.6 cm)
Label: ÉTÉ 1939/Schiaparelli/21.place vendôme Paris
Gift of Mrs. Pauline Potter, 1950
CI 50.34.1

ERIK GUNNAR ASPLUND, Swedish, 1885–1940

ELEVATION OF ADVERTISING MAST FOR
STOCKHOLM EXHIBITION, 1929
Ink and gouache on painted board
H. 24½ x W. 14 in. (62.2 x 35.6 cm)
Edward Pearce Casey Fund, 1984
1984.1168.3

GUGLIEMO ULRICH, Italian, 1904–77

ELEVATION OF FURNITURE SUITE, 1930s
Crayon, colored pencil, and metallic ink over graphite on paper
H. 10⅝ x W. 7⅜ in. (27 x 18.8 cm)
Marked (lower right): ᵂ
Gift of Giancorrado and Giacinta Ulrich, 1989
1989.1105.1

DONALD DESKEY, American, 1894–1989

ARMCHAIR, 1928–29
Chrome-plated steel and reproduction rayon upholstery
H. 28¾ x W. 30 x D. 39½ in. (73 x 76.2 x 100.3 cm)
Manufacturer: Ypsilanti Reed Furniture Company
Purchase, Mr. and Mrs. David Lubart Gift, in memory
of Katherine J. Lubart, 1944–1975, 1979
1979.70a–d

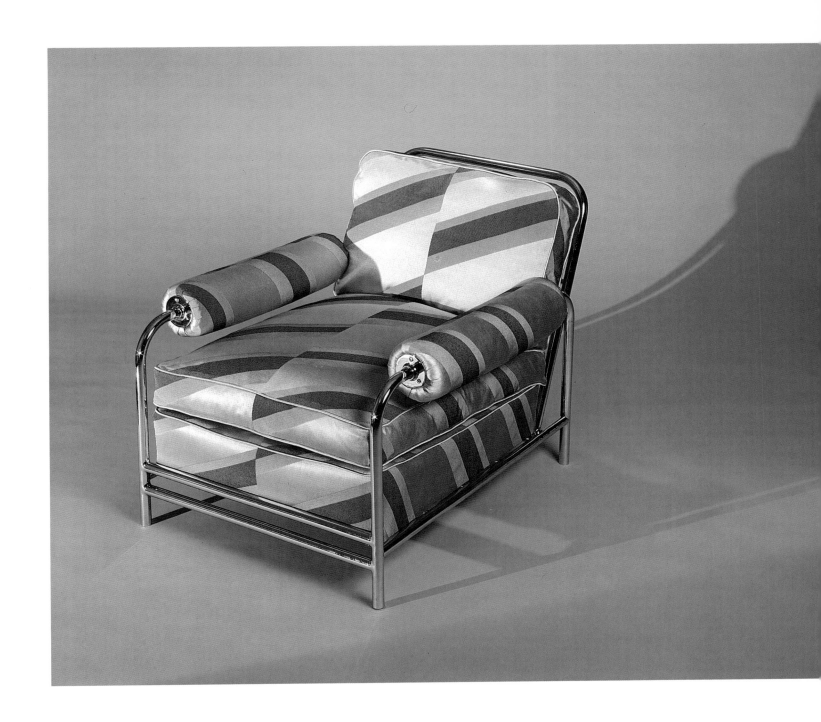

KEM WEBER, American, born Germany, 1889–1963

SIDEBOARD, ca. 1928
Lacquer, silver leaf, and walnut
H. 33⅓ x L. 72¼ x D. 19¾ in. (84.7 x 183.5 x 50.2 cm)
Manufacturer: Grand Rapids Chair Company
Purchase, Theodore R. Gamble, Jr., Gift, in honor of
his mother, Mrs. Theodore Robert Gamble, 1985
1985.86.1

1945

1990

Eero Saarinen, American,
born Finland. Armchair,
ca. 1956

The effects of the Second World War on modern design were as far-ranging as those of the first. Such recent developments cannot be viewed as yet in their full historical perspective, but it may be possible to suggest three major currents that have preoccupied designers and historians during the past four decades: the late stages of Modernism, an increasingly concerted craft movement, and a decisive reaction against Modernism. These ideas will be explored in the five following sections, beginning with late Modernism itself, which may be divided into two phases — an "organic phase" (about 1945 to 1960) and a minimal "geometric phase" (about 1960 to 1990).

Perhaps the most dramatic aftereffect of the war was the end of the cultural hegemony of Europe, in particular England, France, and Germany. The leadership of the Western world clearly passed to the United States, which at long last produced an entire generation of designers of the first rank. The other center of remarkable achievement during these two decades was Scandinavia, which created a distinctive design aesthetic reflective of its socialist experiments.

The Modernist movement, which had arisen in Europe during the 1920s, underwent significant changes as it moved to postwar America. Its socialist utopianism was transformed into a corporate style that reflected an American capitalism and was devoid of any radical political overtones. The hard-edged geometry of the 1920s was softened considerably by the curved forms of moderne and organic designs of the 1930s, and what emerged in the late 1940s was a typically American hybrid mode. A third generation of designers still embraced the ideals of mass production and industrialization, but they used a far more pluralistic vocabulary in terms of form, material, and color.

The principal originators of this organic phase of late Modernism were Charles Eames and Eero Saarinen, who achieved a synthesis as early as 1940 in their revolutionary chairs produced for the Museum of Modern Art competition "Organic Design in Home Furnishings." The technical ability to mold materials into a third dimension allowed the development of a new aesthetic: a sculptural shell supported on an articulated base. For some twenty years, many designers expanded on this idea in plywood, steel, aluminum, and plastic in a multitude of variations. A parallel fascination with sculptural forms may also be noted with such Italians as Gio Ponti and Carlo Mollino, who continued to

Arne Jacobsen, Danish.
Lounge Chair, 1958

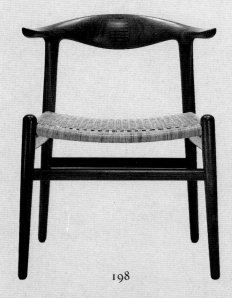

Finn Juhl, Danish.
Settee, 1948

Hans Wegner, Danish.
Side Chair, 1952

develop streamlined or organic designs, as did a number of mainstream American designers in the fifties.

The Scandinavians explored two avenues. On the one hand, there were true industrial designers, including Arne Jacobsen and Verner Panton, who followed the example of Eames and Saarinen. Conversely, there were indigenous "craftsmen-designers," who grew out of the tradition of fine handcraftsmanship that had continued unabated in small workshops throughout Scandinavia, where industrialization had come relatively late. These artists were able to achieve a remarkable synthesis of functionalism and humanism, based in part on the earlier organic mode. This work is best exemplified by the now-classic designs of Finn Juhl and Hans Wegner for wooden chairs — objects that in form, material, and construction combine the old and the new with a chaste perfection.

Regardless of region, this organic phase seems to possess enough stylistic characteristics to constitute a mode, albeit a diversified one. Designers were fascinated, first and foremost, with bold, plastic forms. They favored plain surfaces of natural wood, stainless steel, leather, wool, and marble. Any pattern or texture was inherent in the material, and decorative ornamentation was almost completely absent. American interiors at this time were most often white and gray, accented with primary colors and black; Scandinavians generally used a warmer palette featuring natural woods and textiles.

Whether objects were mass produced or handmade, the quality of construction was remarkably high. A number of aesthetic innovations were made possible by technological advances: foam rubber and stretch fabrics for upholstery, plastic casings for product design, and cast-aluminum frames for furniture. Functional design clearly remained an ideal during the period, but only a few designers — Charles and Ray Eames, most notably — really managed to achieve inexpensive, quality mass production.

The years immediately following World War II were a sanguine period of synthesis and growth, for the mandate of Modernism was still new and diverse enough to accommodate a variety of approaches. By the 1960s, however, a fourth generation of designers would begin to perceive Modernism as a rigid dogma. The issues that had divided the design world in the twenties would surface once again, setting off a fierce debate that would rage for the next quarter of a century.

Verner Panton, Danish. Side Chair, 1960

Kaj Franck, Finnish. "Kremlin Bells" Decanters, 1957

Karl Gustav Hansen, Danish. Pitcher, ca. 1959

TIMO SARPANEVA, Finnish, born 1926

"LANCET" VASE, 1953
Glass
H. 10½ x W. 5¾ x D. 1½ in. (26.7 x 14.6 x 3.8 cm)
Manufacturer: Karhula Ittala Glassworks
Gift of Aarne Simonen, Minister of Commerce and Industry
of Finland, 1956
56.31.3

Peter Voulkos, American, born 1924

Bottle, 1961
Glazed stoneware
H. 18 in. (45.7 cm)
Promised gift of Betty and Monte Factor

HENNING KOPPEL, Danish, 1918–81

SERVER, 1960
Silver
H. 6 x L. 16½ x W. 12 in. (15.2 x 41.9 x 30.5 cm)
Manufacturer: Georg Jensen
Purchase, Edward C. Moore, Jr., Gift, 1961
61.7.11ab

ISAMU NOGUCHI, American, 1904–88

"AKARI E" LAMP, ca. 1966
Handmade mulberry bark paper and bamboo
H. 114 x Diam. 18⅞ in. (289.6 x 47.9 cm)
Manufacturer: Ozeki & Co. Ltd.
Gift of Daniel Wolf, 1990
1990.74

ANNI ALBERS, American, born Germany, 1899

TEXTILE, 1948–49
Sisal, bast fiber, cotton, and Lurex
H. 13½ x W. 17¼ in. (34.3 x 43.8 cm)
Gift of Anni Albers, 1970
1970.75.19

YVES SAINT LAURENT, French, born 1936

COAT, 1960
Wool and plastic
L. (center back) 36 in. (91.4 cm)
House: Christian Dior
Gift of Kay Kerr Uebel, 1981
1981.532.1

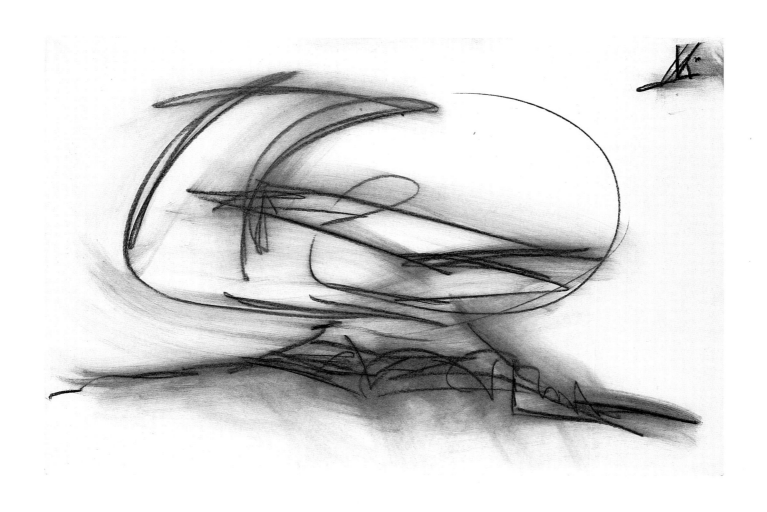

FREDERICK KIESLER, American, born Austria, 1890–1965

ELEVATION OF "ENDLESS HOUSE," 1959
Charcoal on paper
H. 24 x W. 36 in. (61 x 91.4 cm)
Signed (upper right): FK
Edward Pearce Casey Fund, 1979
1979.555

GIO PONTI, Italian, 1891–1979

"POLTRONA TRE PEZZI" (ARMCHAIR IN
THREE PIECES) DRAWING, 1953
Pencil and ink on paper
H. 11 x W. 8¾ in. (27.9 x 22.2 cm)
Gift of Lisa Licitra Ponti, 1990
1990.1044

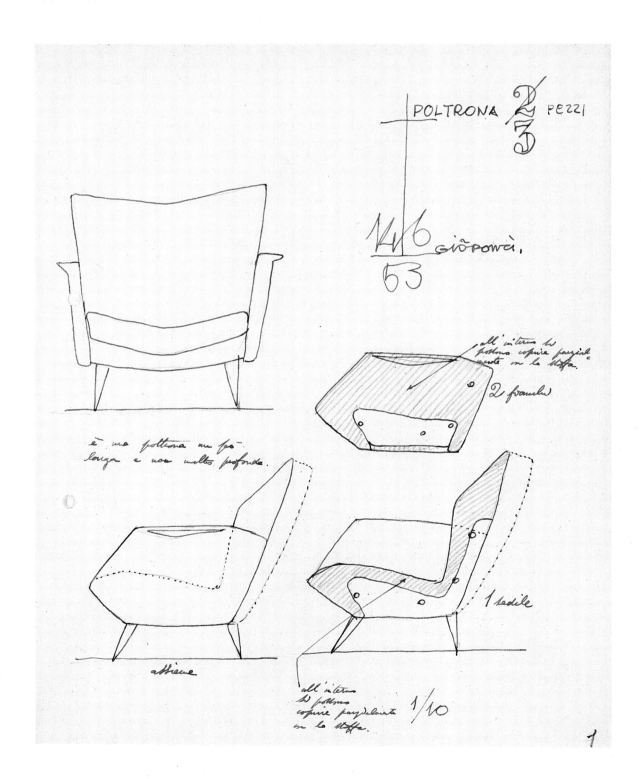

CHARLES ORMOND EAMES, JR., American, 1907–78

RAY EAMES (born Bernice Alexandra Kaiser), American, 1913–88

"DCW" SIDE CHAIR, 1946
Birch plywood, slinkskin, and rubber
H. 28¾ x W. 21⅜ x D. 19½ in. (73 x 54.3 x 49.5 cm)
Manufacturer: Herman Miller Furniture Company
Gift of Mr. and Mrs. I. Wistar Morris III, 1984
1984.556

FINN JUHL, Danish, 1912–89

TABLE, 1950
Teak, maple, and brass
H. 27¾ x L. 83½ x D. 37⅝ in. (70.5 x 212.1 x 95.6 cm)
Manufacturer: Niels Vodder
Purchase, Edward C. Moore, Jr., Gift, 1961
61.7.48

Vico Magistretti,
Italian. "Eclisse"
Lamp, 1967

Despite the various reactions against Modernism, the purist line originating at the Bauhaus had continued largely unbroken, even after the school closed in 1933. Mies van de Rohe, for example, exerted an enormous influence on American architects after World War II, and a third generation of designers — including Poul Kjaerholm, Florence Knoll, and Dieter Rams — perfected their own rigorous, rectilinear aesthetic during this period. Furthermore, the Hochschule für Gestaltung at Ulm (1950–68), under the direction of Max Bill and Tomás Maldonado, revived the Bauhaus's academic program for a time.

The late Modernist work that began to appear in the 1960s from a fourth generation of designers, who were mainly born in the 1930s, was thus part of a long tradition. This group embraced Modernism with remarkable fervor and, perhaps in reaction to the sculptural work of the previous twenty years, carried the Bauhaus ideal of simple geometric form to its ultimate expression. This minimal, geometric phase of late Modernism has continued to the present time. Though widely divergent in scale, the black glass skyscraper and the Zanuso-Sapper black cubic television remain among the ultimate icons of this reductionist art.

Initially, the primary center for this design was Milan. Seeking a lucrative international market, Italian manufacturers commissioned architects like Mario Bellini, Vico Magistretti, and Tobia Scarpa to design their luxury products. Following the Scandinavian model, Italian companies remained small, relying on a combination of machine- and hand-production. This enabled innovative firms such as Artemide, Cassina, Danese, and Kartell to produce a wide range of quality objects for a market whose tastes changed quickly.

During the 1980s Milan was challenged by an emerging generation of Japanese designers, including Toshiyuki Kita, Masayuki Kurokawa, and Shigeru Uchida, many of whom had worked at one time in Milan. These designers have continued the minimal

Tassilo von Grolman,
German. "Mono" Teapot
and Stand, 1981

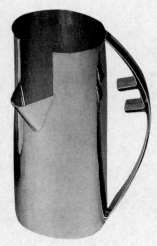

Carlo Scarpa, Italian.
Carafe, ca. 1974

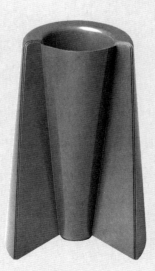

Enzo Mari, Italian.
Vase, 1969

Roseline Delisle, Canadian.
"Serie Pneumatique 36"
Covered Jar, 1987

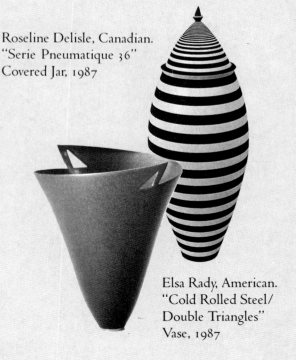

Elsa Rady, American.
"Cold Rolled Steel/
Double Triangles"
Vase, 1987

aesthetic of late Modernism in a refined fusion of Eastern and Western motifs, most notably in the treatment of the Western chair as an abstract sculptural form.

The underlying factor of this reductionist mode is surely the use of geometry as a symbol of order and as a genesis of form. Compositions tend to be elemental with a minimum of parts; objects thus impart little sense of scale with the absence of the traditional division into bottom, middle, and top.

Within such a limited aesthetic, a highly finished surface becomes of prime importance. Designers have often sought to express the "essence" of a material — be it steel, glass, or plastic — by exaggerating the qualities of a substance to the ultimate. The palette generally consists of minimal compositions of black, white, or gray, sometimes combined with metallic finishes or primary colors. Pattern and ornament of any kind are avoided.

In theory, technology continues to be seen as a major progenitor of this late Modernist mode. Designers are eager to employ new materials and manufacturing innovations, such as rigid plastics, polyurethane, and injection molding. In reality, however, the result is often not so much an "honest" expression of material or function as a rarified statement of an artistic idea.

In a century noted for its rapid changes in fashion, it is remarkable that Modernism has remained a vital force for nearly seven decades. What is most commendable about this latest generation of adherents is that it has recaptured to a great degree the spirit and purity of Modernism's originators. A style of such longevity, on the other hand, invariably runs the risk of appearing to be aseptic, which indeed proved to be true for a number of designers who have charted a completely antithetical course — one now called Post-Modernism.

Masayuki Kurokawa, Japanese.
"Domani" Lamp, 1976

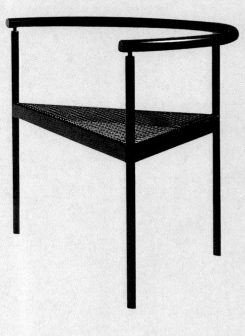

Shigeru Uchida, Japanese.
"September" Armchair, 1973

Mario Botta, Swiss.
"Seconda" Armchair, 1982

Mario Bellini, Italian.
"Break" Armchair, 1976

ACHILLE CASTIGLIONI, Italian, born 1918

"OVIO" GLASSES AND CARAFE, 1983
Glass and rubber
Carafe: H. 11⅜ x Diam. 2¾ in. (28.9 x 7 cm)
Manufacturer: Danese
Gift of Jacqueline and Bruno Danese, 1988
1988.184.9a–f

GEERT LAP, Dutch, born 1951

VESSELS, 1989
Earthenware
Left: H. 6⅞ x Diam. 6¼ in. (17.5 x 15.9 cm)
Gift of Claes Oldenburg and Coosje van Bruggen, 1990
1990.71.1,2

Mario Bellini, Italian, born 1935

Tea and Coffee Service
(prototype), 1980
Silver, rose quartz, and lapis lazuli
Tray: H. 1½ x W. 19¾ x D. 19¾ in.
(3.8 x 50.2 x 50.2 cm)
Manufacturer: Cleto Munari
Gift of Cleto Munari, 1988, 1990
1988.191.6, 1990.1.96.1ab–4ab

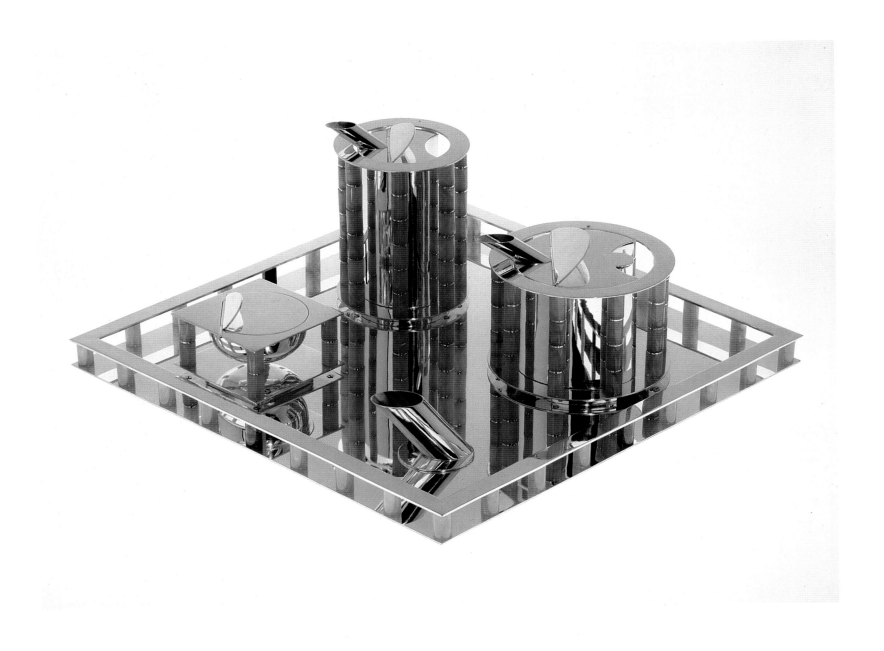

RICHARD SAPPER, German, born 1932

"TIZIO" LAMP, 1973
Aluminum, thermoplastic, and metal alloy
H. 46½ x Diam. 4⅜ in. (118.1 x 11.1 cm)
Manufacturer: Artemide S.p.A.
Gift of Artemide S.p.A., 1988
1988.236.9

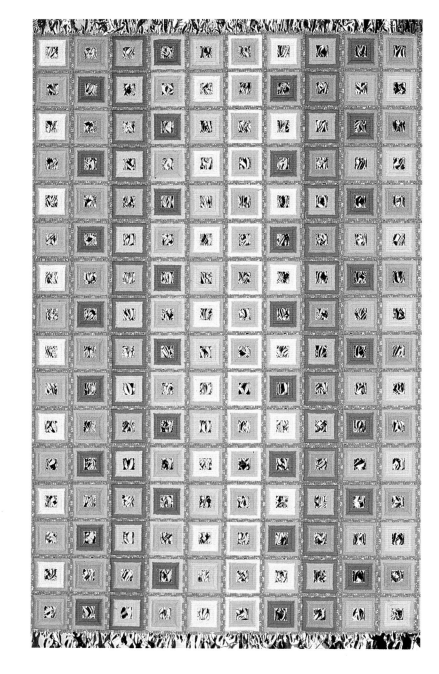

Jack Lenor Larsen, American, born 1927

"Magnum Golden" Textile (detail), 1972
Wool, nylon, acrylic, and Mylar
L. 55½ x W. 53½ in. (141 x 135.9 cm)
Manufacturer: Jack Lenor Larsen, Inc.
Gift of Jack Lenor Larsen, 1984
1984.242.9

ANDRÉ COURRÈGES, French, born 1923

DRESS AND JACKET, 1965
Wool, silk, and plastic
Dress: L. (center back) 36 in. (91.4 cm)
Label: COURREGES/PARIS/Made in France
Gift of Kimberly Knitwear, Inc., 1974
1974.136.5ab

TADAO ANDO, Japanese, born 1941

PLAN OF NAKANOSHIMA PROJECT, OSAKA,
JAPAN, 1980
Crayon on lithograph
H. 33 x W. 69¼ in. (83.8 x 175.9 cm)
Gift of Tadao Ando, 1988
1988.1116

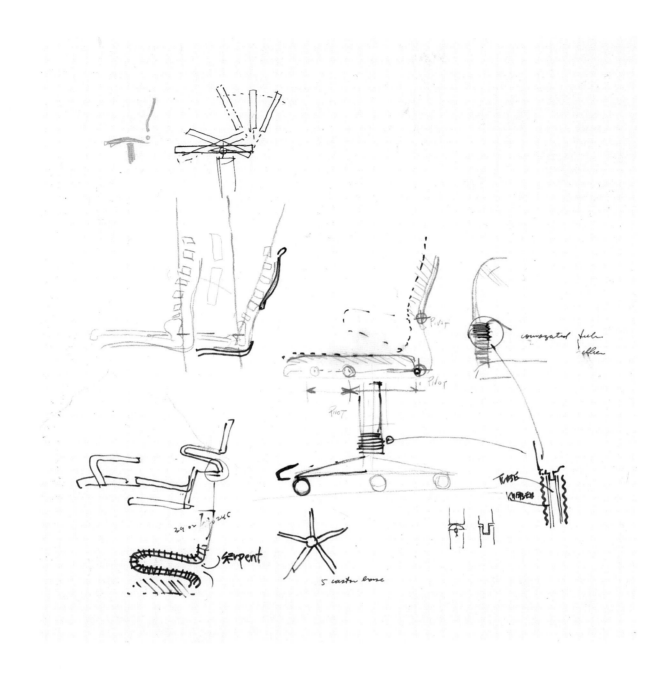

Emilio Ambasz, Argentinian, born 1943

Preliminary Sketches for
"Vertebra" Chair (detail), 1974–75
Pencil and ink on paper
H. 20¼ x W. 14⅞ in. (51.4 x 37.8 cm)
Gift of Emilio Ambasz, 1990
1990.1022

Joe Colombo, Italian, 1930–71

"Tube" Chair, 1970
Plastic, polyurethane, and synthetic knit upholstery
Largest tube: H. 25¼ x Diam. 19⅜ in. (64.1 x 49.2 cm)
Manufacturer: Flexform
Purchase, Theodore R. Gamble, Jr., Gift, in honor of
his mother, Mrs. Theodore Robert Gamble, 1987
1987.98.1a–d

Disassembled modular units

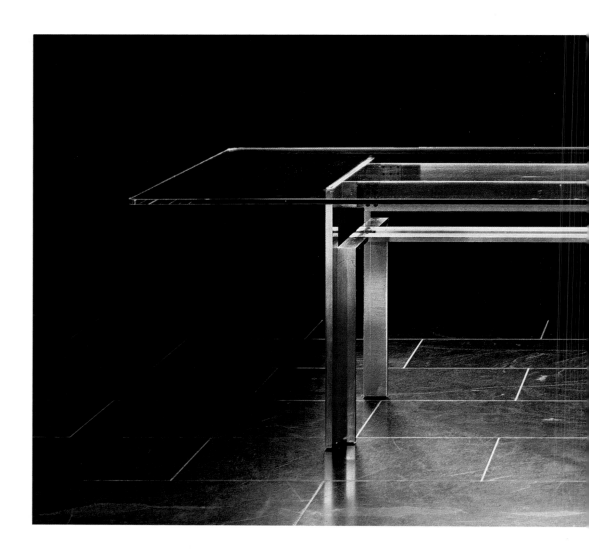

CARLO SCARPA, Italian, 1906–78

"DOGE 306" TABLE, 1969
Glass, steel, and brass
H. 28 x W. 120 x D. 40 in. (71.1 x 304.8 x 101.6 cm)
Manufacturer: Simon International
Gift of Simon International S.p.A., 1989
1989.404

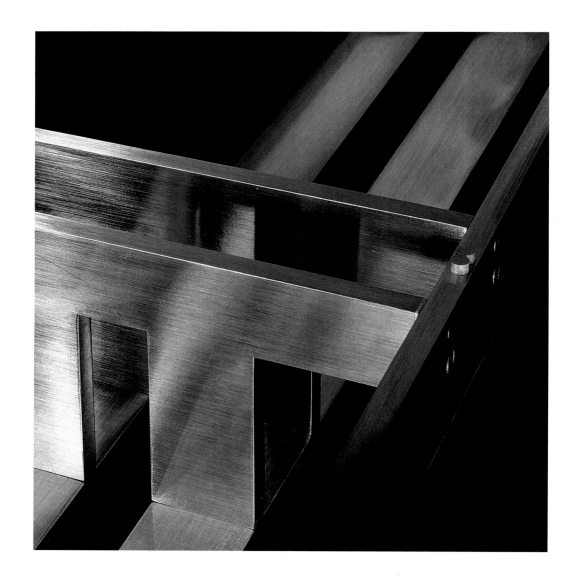

Detail of center stretchers

Detail of intersecting stretchers and legs

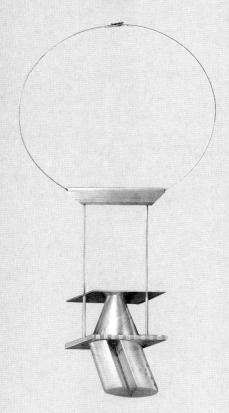

Claus Bury, German.
Necklace, 1975

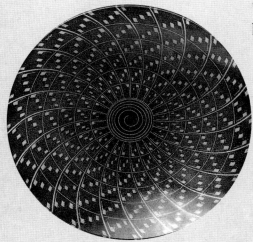

Maurice Heaton, American.
Plate, 1949

Earlier sections have dealt with stylistic modes that consisted largely of decorative or industrial design; handcrafted objects — such as glass, ceramics, or textiles — were illustrated in each, however, because craft has traditionally constituted an integral part of the applied arts. Before World War II, craftsmen most often worked within these two areas, frequently as collaborators with designers or painters and sculptors. This section deals with a major development in postwar applied arts — an intellectual and aesthetic shift in which craft has assumed a position independent of the two other design areas.

During this century the craft movement has in many ways found its greatest acceptance in America, where there had long been an emphasis on the individual and handwork. Until the Second World War, though, the field remained highly fragmented and regional in scope. From that time, a more focused national movement came into being with the founding of what are currently known as the American Craft Council (1939), *American Craft* magazine (1941), and the American Craft Museum (1956). At last craftsmen had a multiple forum for debating and sharing their work. The establishment in 1964 of the World Crafts Council and its international conferences provided further structure for a burgeoning movement.

These organizational endeavors paralleled other changes in the field. Craft was evolving into a "high art." Craftsmen were no longer merely skilled artisans but were now formally educated at universities, invariably in fine-arts departments, rather than at schools of architecture or design. This transcendence of craft into fine art has been accelerated more recently by the large number of international galleries and museums actively promoting craftsmen as major artists. The craftman's ultimate goal, of course, was to be accepted as the artistic equal of decorative and industrial designers, as well as of painters and sculptors.

While there were earlier precedents for this new conception of the craftsman as

Ann Warff, Swedish.
"Leben Lassen" Bowl, 1981

Sam Maloof, American.
Settee #3/87, 1987

artist — George Ohr or Bernard Leach, for example — it was only after World War II that these ideas coalesced into a large-scale movement. Such fundamental changes in the field have led to a protean rather than a monolithic situation, in which the majority of craftsmen may be divided into two distinct camps: those who continue the long tradition of making functional objects and those who create non-utilitarian objects as works of fine art.

Any design current seeking to establish itself as a major movement must define its own standards of quality and create an historical context. It is symptomatic of the contemporary craft field — at least at this moment in time — that it appears to exist largely in an intellectual and stylistic vacuum; the absence of comprehensive collections and scholarly studies has contributed greatly to this inconstant state. Fine-arts craftsmen, who have few real antecedents, are often reduced to searching desultorily for inspiration in painting and sculpture. Functional craftsmen, on the other hand, frequently turn in on themselves, focusing myopically on their own media.

In terms of functional craft itself, this situation has resulted in a common attitude rather than a style. Certainly one of the most cherished ideals has been the individual artist in his studio — versus a large workshop with assistants doing serial productions — where one-of-a-kind objects could be created for everyday use at moderate cost. Functional craft, as such, tends to become an autodidactic discipline, where the emphasis is placed on the extension of traditional forms, the mastery of materials, and the perfecting of technical skills. This has led to the cult of the craftsman spending his life completely within one medium, free of extrinsic influence. The ultimate criterion for judging work thus becomes the individual development of the artist rather than any larger framework relating to twentieth-century culture as a whole. Hence this section does not share a stylistic theme but rather celebrates the remarkable achievements of ten individual artists.

Toshiko Takeazu, American. "Sakura" Vase (top) and "Air" Vase, 1967

Michael Jerry, American. Cooking Pot, 1975

Karen Karnes, American. Covered Jar, 1980–85

Ron Kent, American. Bowl, 1982

KLAUS MOJE, German, born 1936

DISH, 1979
Fused glass
H. 2¾ x Diam. 17⅝ in. (7 x 44.8 cm)
Gift of Douglas and Annie Heller and Dale Chihuly, 1980
1980.142

BERNARD LEACH, British, 1887–1979

BOTTLE, ca. 1958
Stoneware
H. 14⅞ x Diam. 7 in. (37.8 x 17.8 cm)
Rogers Fund, 1960
1960.46

MARGARET WITHERS CRAVER, American, born 1907

BOWL, 1961
Gold and en-résille enamel
H. 4½ x W. 4½ x D. 4⅞ in. (11.4 x 11.4 x 12.4 cm)
Gift of Mrs. Alfred Slade Mills, 1983
1983.361

GEORGE NAKASHIMA, American, 1905–90

"KENT HALL" LAMP, ca. 1964
English walnut, rosewood, holly, and fiberglass
H. 60 x Diam. 16½ in. (152.4 x 41.9 cm)
Promised gift of Dr. and Mrs. Charles Hardy

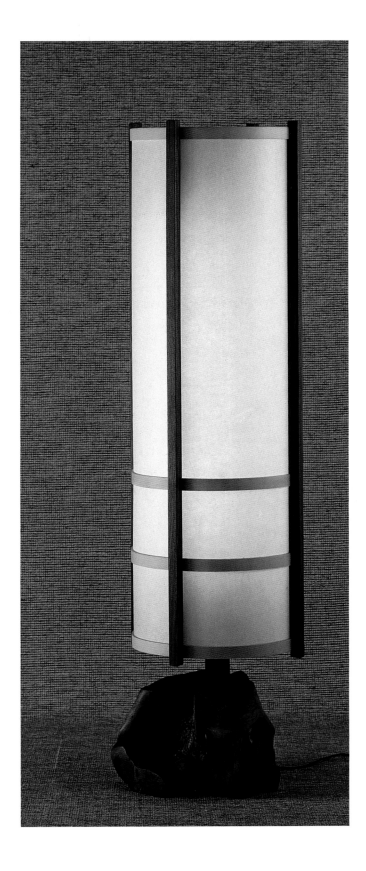

OLGA DE AMARAL, Colombian, born 1937

"ALQUIMIA XIII" HANGING, 1984
Cotton, linen, rice paper, gesso, paint, and gold leaf
L. 71 x W. 29½ in. (180.3 x 74.9 cm)
Gift of Olga and Jim Amaral
1987.387

Detail of figural panel on back

NORMA MINKOWITZ, American, born 1937

    SWEATER, 1974
    Cotton
    L. 32 in. (81.3 cm)
    Gift of Norma Minkowitz, 1980
    1980.49

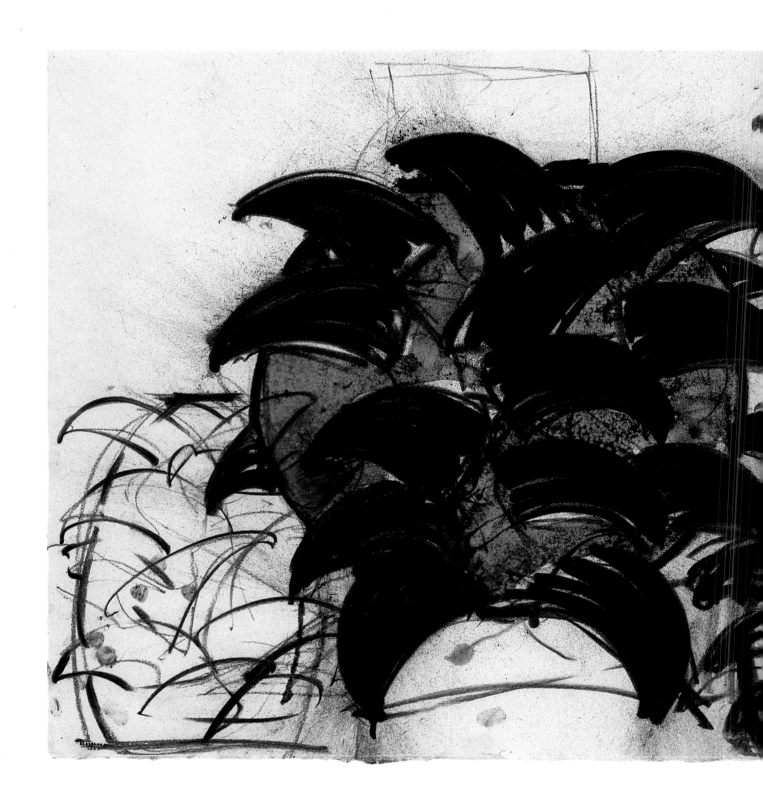

DALE CHIHULY, American, born 1941

ELEVATION STUDIES FOR "VENETIAN SERIES"
GLASS VASES, 1988
Charcoal and watercolor on paper
H. 22⅜ x W. 30⅛ in. (56.8 x 76.5 cm)
Signed in pencil (lower right): Chihuly.88
Gift of Charles Cowles, 1989
1989.1137.1

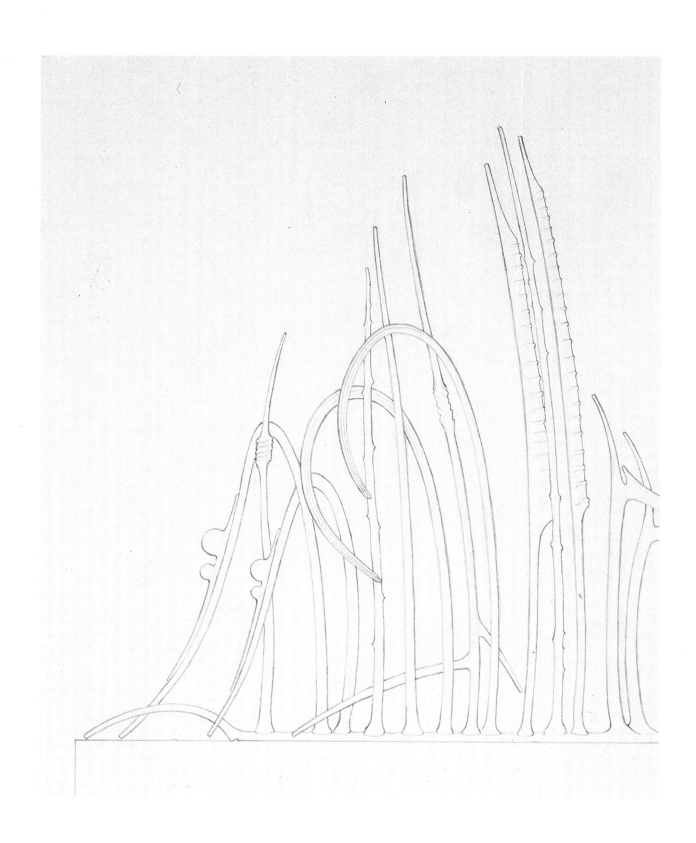

ALBERT PALEY, American, born 1944

PRELIMINARY ELEVATIONS OF IRONWORK FOR STAIRWELL ENCLOSURE, 1983
Designed for Hyatt Regency Grand Cypress Hotel, Orlando, Florida
Graphite on paper
H. 29 x W. 23 in. (73.7 x 58.4 cm)
Signed (lower right): Albert Paley 8–83
Gift of Grand Cypress Hotel Corporation, a subsidiary of
Dutch Institutional Holding Company, 1990
1990.1021

WENDELL CASTLE, American, born 1932

"Two-Seater" Settee, ca. 1977
Cherry
H. 30½ x W. 60½ x D. 38 in. (77.5 x 153.7 x 96.5 cm)
Gift of Dr. and Mrs. Irwin R. Berman, 1977
1977.225

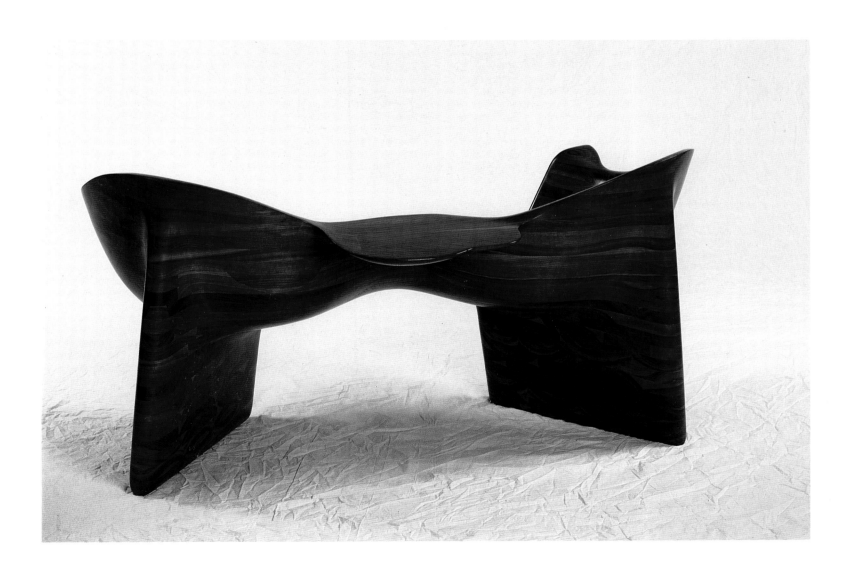

WHARTON ESHERICK, American, 1887–1970

MUSIC STAND, 1962
Cherry
H. 43 x W. 19½ x D. 16 in. (109.2 x 49.5 x 40.6 cm)
Gift of Dr. Irwin R. Berman, in memory of his father,
Allan Lake Berman, 1979
1979.320

Achille and Pier Giacomo
Castiglioni, Italian.
"Taccia" Lamp, 1962

Robert A. M. Stern,
American. "Metropolitan"
Candlestick, 1984

True to cyclical fashion, Modernism evolved in time from the avant-garde to the mainstream, and by the late 1950s and early sixties outré designers elected to explore antithetical approaches to this rationalist aesthetic. The reaction against Modernism was at first a diffuse and peripheral movement; its evolution into a true style, in fact, required almost two decades.

One of the early manifestations of this Post-Modernist reaction occurred in England during the 1950s with such theorists as Reyner Banham and the Independent Group. They advocated that design concepts did not have to derive a priori from architectural principles; rather, design could exist as a separate discipline with an independent theoretical basis. They contended that the application of rationalist criteria was particularly inappropriate to such a pragmatic field largely subject to the forces of mass production. Drawing on the precedent set by the moderne designers of the 1930s, these early advocates wished to place a greater emphasis on symbolism, styling, and expendability. The machine aesthetic was thus replaced by popular culture as a basis for design.

At about the same time in America, formalist architects such as Edward Durell Stone and Philip Johnson instigated a revival of interest in neoclassical motifs, which enjoyed a brief vogue. This work had little in the way of real, theoretical underpinnings, and certainly no attempt was made to produce unified interiors with furnishings. By the mid-1960s, though, Robert Venturi offered a serious intellectual basis for questioning Modernist tenets in his book *Complexity and Contradiction in Architecture* (1966). Equally important were the monumental buildings of Louis Kahn, which drew in a highly original way on Classical and Neoclassical sources. This American reaction to Modernism remained largely an architectural phenomenon, with the exception of such designers as Charles and Ray Eames, whose renewed interest in ornament, color, and pattern was confined to their interiors, exhibitions, and films rather than industrial designs.

The most pronounced response in the applied arts occurred in Italy, where radical designers in the turbulent 1960s equated Modernism with an affluent capitalist society. The highly polemical designs created initially by groups such as Archizoom and Superstudio, and individuals such as Ettore Sottsass and Gaetano Pesce, were in many

Hans Hollein, Austrian.
Compote, ca. 1980

Robert Venturi,
American. "Grandmother"
Dinnerware, 1984

Stanley Tigerman,
American. "Pompeii"
Dinnerware, 1984

ways more interesting for their intellectual concepts than their aesthetic achievement. They constituted, however, a major catalyst for things to come.

By the mid-1970s, all of these reactions coalesced into a coherent movement, one that quickly became an international — though not doctrinaire — force. Two major directions in Post-Modernism may be noted: an eclectic historical revival and a highly subjective, anti-rationalist stance. Each was very different in terms of form, theory, and objective.

Historicism had been a basic tenet of the Modern movement since its inception. Its timeless appeal lay in the sense of order it provided, for change may often be more easily accommodated within a recognized style. For many of these outré designers, a renewal of the decorative tradition of the 1920s with its emphasis on historical form, luxurious materials, and craftsmanship offered a viable alternative to industrial design. Of greatest importance was their desire to reassert humanist values — versus the machine aesthetic — as a new basis for design.

While the variety of stylistic sources has ranged from the Art Nouveau, Wiener Werkstätte, and Art Déco in this century back to the Renaissance and Classical worlds, there are a number of common characteristics. These revivalist designers tend to prefer subtly modeled forms with clearly delineated parts. A sense of solid mass is lightened by an emphasis on smooth, polished finishes. Traditional materials — such as exotic veneers, stone, silver, silk, or engraved glass — are used to express their sensuous rather than constructive quality, and color, pattern, and ornament are used in a decorative though integrated manner. New technology may be used to duplicate the effects of earlier techniques or materials, as for example with silk-screening and printed plastic laminates, but the main emphasis is placed on the revival of traditional handcrafted skills. Likewise, the primary criterion here is one of style in a formalist sense, rather than function or economy.

This historical revival, initially an architectural movement, spread by the early 1980s to all areas of the applied arts. Its principal proponents remain architects such as Michael Graves, Hans Hollein, and Arata Isozaki. Its overriding goal — the renewal of decorative form, material, and craftsmanship—remains a major issue for late-twentieth-century design.

Mario Botta, Swiss.
"Shogun" Lamp, 1986

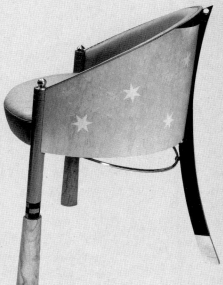

Norbert Berghof, Michael Landes, and Wolfgang Rang, German. "Frankfurter Stuhl F III" Armchair, 1985–86

Michael Graves, American.
GQ Manstyle Award Cup
and Lounge Chair, 1982

RICHARD MEIER, American, born 1934

STEMWARE, 1984
Left to right: "Manhattan" (prototype), "Lattice"
(prototype), "Highball" (prototype), and "Professor"
(production piece)
Engraved glass
Goblet at right: H. 9⅞ x Diam. 2⅞ in. (25.1 x 7.3 cm)
Manufacturer: Swid Powell
Gift of Swid Powell, 1985
1985.199.9–12

BETTY WOODMAN, American, born 1930

"PILLOW" PITCHER, 1981
Glazed earthenware
H. 19¾ x W. 22 x D. 13 in. (50.2 x 55.9 x 33 cm)
Promised gift of Mrs. Larry Horner

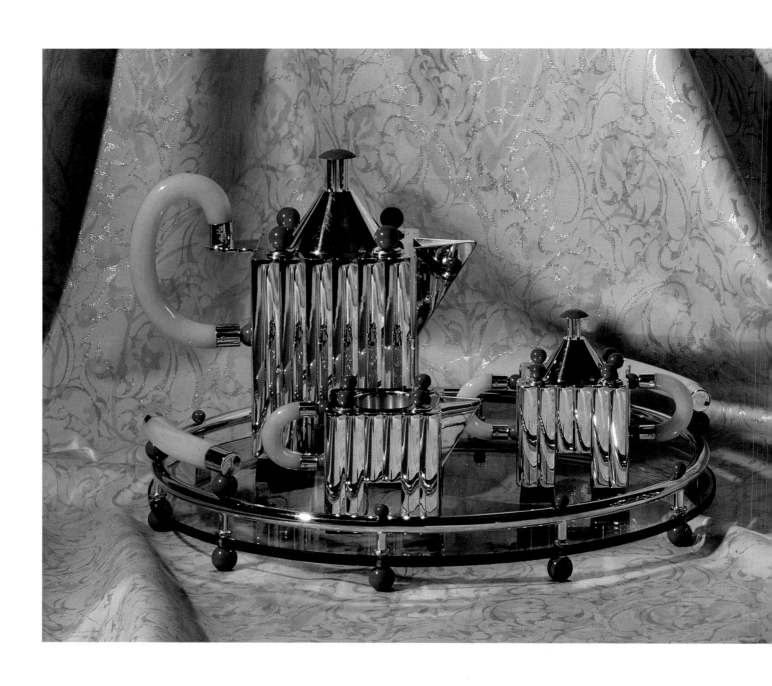

MICHAEL GRAVES, American, born 1934

TEA AND COFFEE SERVICE
(prototype), 1980–83
800 silver, lacquered aluminum, mock ivory,
and Bakelite
Tray: H. 3½ x Diam. 16 in. (8.9 x 40.6 cm)
Manufacturer: Officina Alessi, Alessi S.p.A.
Promised gift of Diane, Daniel,
and Mathew Wolf

Aulenti lamp telescoped

GAE AULENTI, Italian, born 1927

"PIPISTRELLO" LAMP, 1965
Lacquered aluminum, stainless steel, and perspex
H. 27¾ x Diam. 21¼ in. (70.5 x 54 cm)
Manufacturer: Martinelli Luce
Gift of Martinelli Luce, 1989
1989.401

SHEILA HICKS, American, born 1934

"PALM" TAPESTRY, 1984–85
Prototype of tapestry for King Saud University, Riyadh,
Saudi Arabia
Wool, cotton, rayon, silk, and linen
L. 143½ x W. 108½ in. (364.5 x 275.6 cm)
Manufacturer: Atelier Philippe Hecquet
Anonymous Gift, 1986
1986.298

ISSEY MIYAKE, Japanese, born 1938

DRESS AND WRAP, 1977
Silk-screened silk
Dress: L. (center back) 56¼ in. (142.9 cm)
House: Issey Miyake
Back printed with design, "The Creation,"
by Tadanori Yokoo
Gift of Issey Miyake, 1977
1977.405.9ab

ARATA ISOZAKI, Japanese, born 1931

EXTERIOR PERSPECTIVE OF THE MUSEUM OF
CONTEMPORARY ART, LOS ANGELES, 1983
Pencil and colored pencils on tracing paper
H. 9½ x W. 10½ in. (24.1 x 26.7 cm)
Signed (lower right): Arata Isozaki
Edward Pearce Casey Fund, 1987
1987.1020

ROBERT VENTURI, American, born 1925

ELEVATIONS OF "ART DÉCO" SIDE CHAIR, 1982
Detail of full elevation (left): Graphite, black marker,
colored markers, and paper collage on tracing paper
H. 56½ x W. 36 in. (143.5 x 91.4 cm)
Signed (lower left): Robert Venturi: '82
Detail elevation (above): Graphite and black marker on
tracing paper
H. 27½ x W. 29 in. (69.9 x 73.7 cm)
Signed (lower right): Robert Venturi: '82
Gift of Venturi, Rauch and Scott Brown, 1984
1984.568.1,2

SHIRO KURAMATA, Japanese, born 1934

"How High the Moon" Armchair, 1986
Nickel-plated steel
H. 28¼ x W. 37⅜ x D. 32 in. (71.8 x 94.9 x 81.3 cm)
Manufacturer: Vitra Inc.
Gift of Vitra Inc., Basel, Switzerland, 1988
1988.186

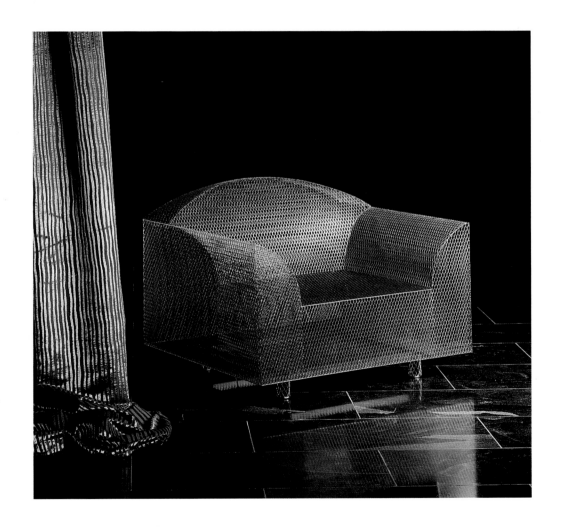

Oscar Tusquets Blanca, Spanish, born 1941

"Alada 985" Table (prototype), 1985
Painted wood, bronze, and etched glass
H. 27⅞ x W. 79 x D. 43¾ in.
(70.8 x 200.7 x 111.1 cm)
Manufacturer: Casas
Gift of Casas-Barcelona, 1990
1990.68

Detail of foot

Harvey Littleton, American. "Amber Crested Form" Sculpture, 1976

At mid-century another group of Post-Modernist designers became increasingly alarmed by the global spread of Western capitalism and, like the Arts and Crafts Movement of a century earlier, assumed the role of the artist as reformer of society. Confronting the exigent issues of worldwide industrialization and urbanization, these artists wished to reassert the importance of the individual, and they began a quixotic search for a new humanism that was to be highly iconoclastic and subjective. This particular Post-Modernist reaction developed during the 1960s in centers as far apart as Berkeley and Milan, in a milieu of rock music, blue jeans, and anti-war protests. It has evolved into two segments linked both aesthetically and intellectually: non-functional craftsmen and anti-rationalist designers.

Perhaps the earliest manifestation occurred in the craft field; wishing to break out of the category of craftsman, these artists moved into painting and sculpture in search of a new formal and intellectual basis for their work, a direction often referred to as the Studio Movement. Momentous changes took place almost simultaneously through all the craft media in America during the 1960s and within the next decade spread to Europe and Japan. Many artists moved away from a preoccupation with practical, one-of-a-kind objects toward a larger conception of their work as theoretical and serial, necessitating large studios and assistants. Moreover, technique, a fundamental aspect of functional craft, was often given less importance than the intellectual concept of the object. Some artists, especially on the West Coast, began to assume a highly polemical and confrontational attitude in their work. Ironically, a parallel movement was occurring at the same time among a number of sculptors and painters who were creating applied objects devoid of any design criteria. This disintegration of the boundaries between design and fine art had its roots in the 1930s.

As for the anti-rationalists, again the most pronounced reaction occurred in Italy. Several groups and individuals had sought an alternate direction to Modernist design in the 1960s, but by the 1970s their efforts coalesced into a major force, often referred to as the Anti-Design Movement. Among the most influential groups were Studio Alchimia and Memphis; the latter, in particular, had an explosive impact on international design in the 1980s with its radical new concepts of form, pattern, and color. These Post-

Tom Patti, American. "Banded Flair" Bottle, 1976

Wayne Higby, American. "Winter Inlet" Ceramic, 1976

Françoise Grossen, Swiss. "Grasshopper" Textile, ca. 1975

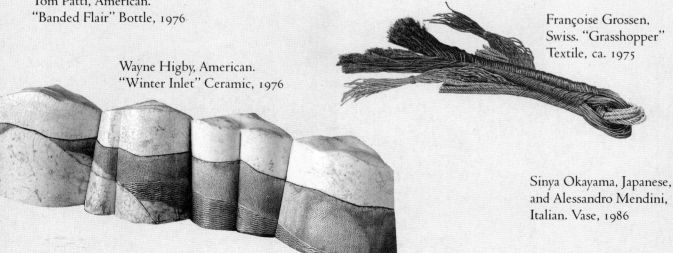

Sinya Okayama, Japanese, and Alessandro Mendini, Italian. Vase, 1986

Modernists initially worked in the applied arts and only subsequently received large architectural commissions.

Such a highly individualistic and antithetical movement is not easy to codify, yet there are certain traits shared by its proponents. For one, the applied arts are not considered in purely formalist terms but are viewed as a vehicle for social commentary, often utopian in tone. Overt references are frequently made to past and contemporary fine art, especially nihilistic movements like Dada. This aspect of Post-Modernism may be described as one that celebrates richness and complexity: form over function, the decorative over the industrial, the intuitive over the rational, and pluralism over universal verities.

In reaction to the "good design" of the Modernists, mass culture was venerated over high art. Artists deliberately used vernacular forms, common materials, and crude craftsmanship as elements in their work. Pop Art, 1950s kitsch, and Las Vegas suggested a new iconography that artists could incorporate into either sophisticated or deliberately vulgar designs. These works were often characterized by an underlying sense of impermanence and disorder.

Such anti-rationalist design tends to feature complex and exaggerated sculptural forms free of functional constraints. Materials are often used in surprising combinations: wire mesh, plastic laminates, or cardboard paired with marble or exotic veneers. Color, pattern, and ornament are treated as equal elements in relation to form — often at a baroque intensity. Technology is of secondary importance, for materials are not used so much in a constructive as in an emotive sense. Anti-rationalist design has generally been of limited production, requiring considerable handwork; this has in turn led to a reliance on small workshops for fabrication and art galleries for distribution.

These Post-Modernists began by protesting the existing order but have now become an established movement. Their utopian vision, like that of William Morris and his contemporaries, has been to unite the fine and applied arts but, especially, to make design an integral part of daily existence. As we approach the end of the twentieth century, they remind us once again of the fundamental power of design — the most accessible of all the arts — to ennoble and enrich our everyday lives.

Superstudio, Italian. "Gherpe" Lamp, ca. 1967

Ettore Sottsass, Italian, born Austria. "The Structures Tremble" Table, 1979

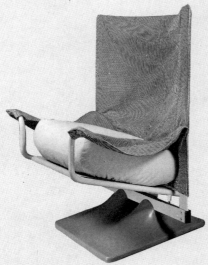

Archizoom, Italian. "AEO" Armchair, 1987

Gaetano Pesce, Italian. "Sit Down" Lounge Chair, 1975

Stanislav Libensky, Czechoslovakian, born 1921

Jaroslava Brychtova, Czechoslovakian, born 1924

"Bride Table" Sculpture, 1989
Safirin glass
H. 9 x W. 18⅛ x D. 7⅛ in. (22.9 x 46 x 18.1 cm)
Purchase, James R. Houghton Gift, 1990
1990.8

Reverse view of "Bride Table"

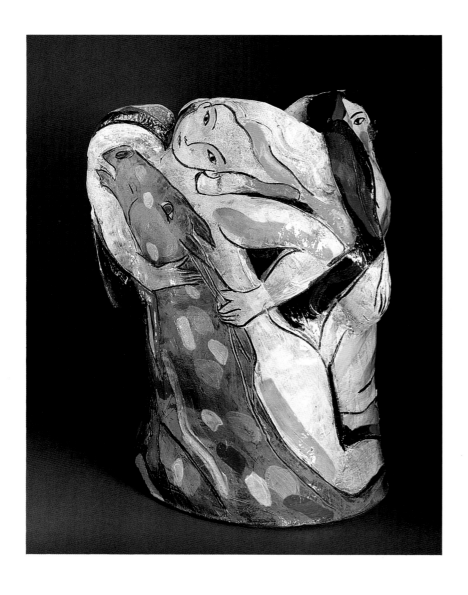

Views of "Blue Mountain Horses," moving counterclockwise

Rudy Autio, American, born 1926

"Blue Mountain Horses" Sculpture, 1984
Stoneware
H. 29¼ x Diam. 22¾ in. (74.3 x 57.8 cm)
Promised gift of Emily Fisher Landau

CHUNGHI CHOO, American, born Korea, 1938

CENTERPIECE, 1979
Silver-plated copper and plexiglass
H. 11⅛ x W. 18¾ x D. 6¼ in. (28.3 x 47.6 x 15.9 cm)
Gift of Jack Lenor Larsen, 1980
1980.580.ab

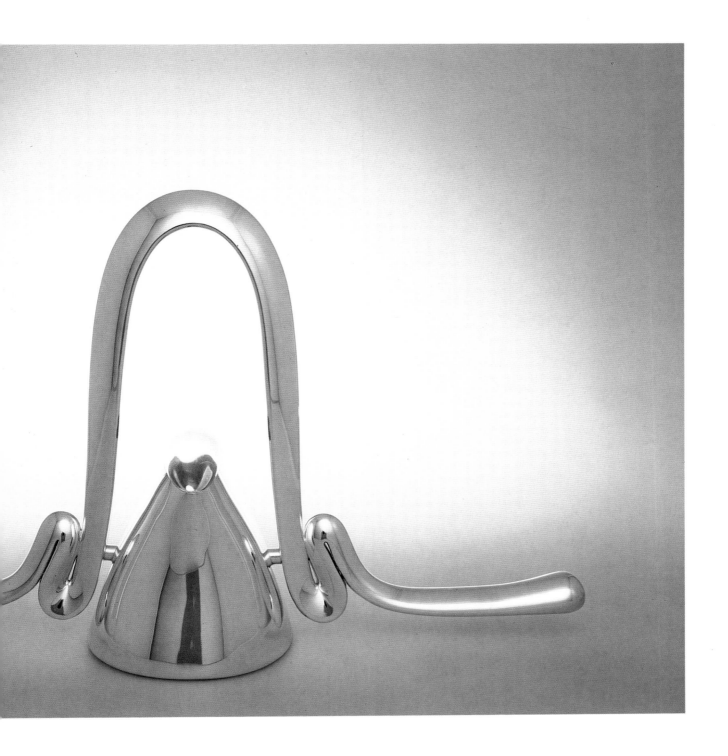

FRANK GEHRY, American, born Canada, 1929

"FISH" LAMP, 1983–84
Steel, wood, colorcore Formica plastic laminate,
and electric lights
H. 71 x W. 29 x D. 29 in. (180.3 x 73.7 x 73.7 cm)
Manufacturer: New City Editions
Promised gift of Stephan I. Montifiore

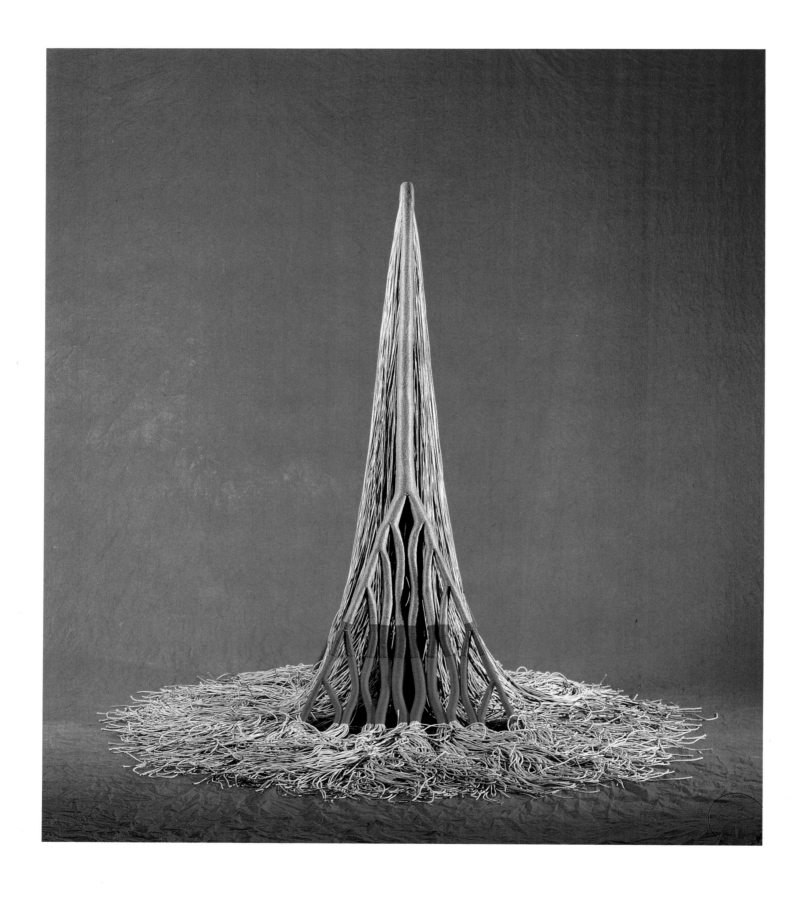

CLAIRE ZEISLER, American, born 1903

"TRI-COLOR ARCH" FIBER
CONSTRUCTION, 1983–84
Hemp and synthetic fiber
H. 74 in. (188 cm)
Gift of the artist, 1987
1987.371

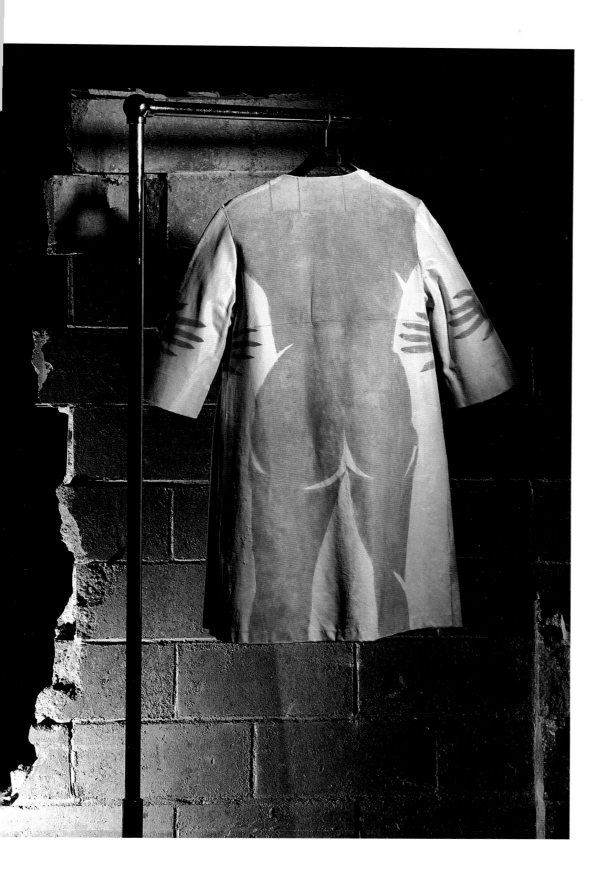

JACQUES KAPLAN (designer),
    American, born 1924

MARISOL (born Marisol Escobar; painter),
    American, born France, 1930

COAT, 1960
Painted calfskin and mink
L. (center back) 40½ in. (102.9 cm)
Manufacturer: Jacques Kaplan
Gift of Pascal Kaplan, Ph.D., 1979
1979.570.1

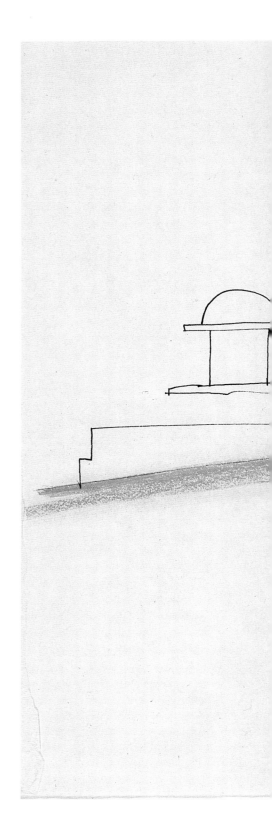

ETTORE SOTTSASS, JR., Italian, born Austria, 1917

ELEVATION OF DANIEL WOLF RESIDENCE,
RIDGWAY, COLORADO, 1986
Graphite, colored pencil, and oil pastel on paper
H. 11 x W. 14 in. (27.9 x 35.6 cm)
Promised gift of Daniel Wolf

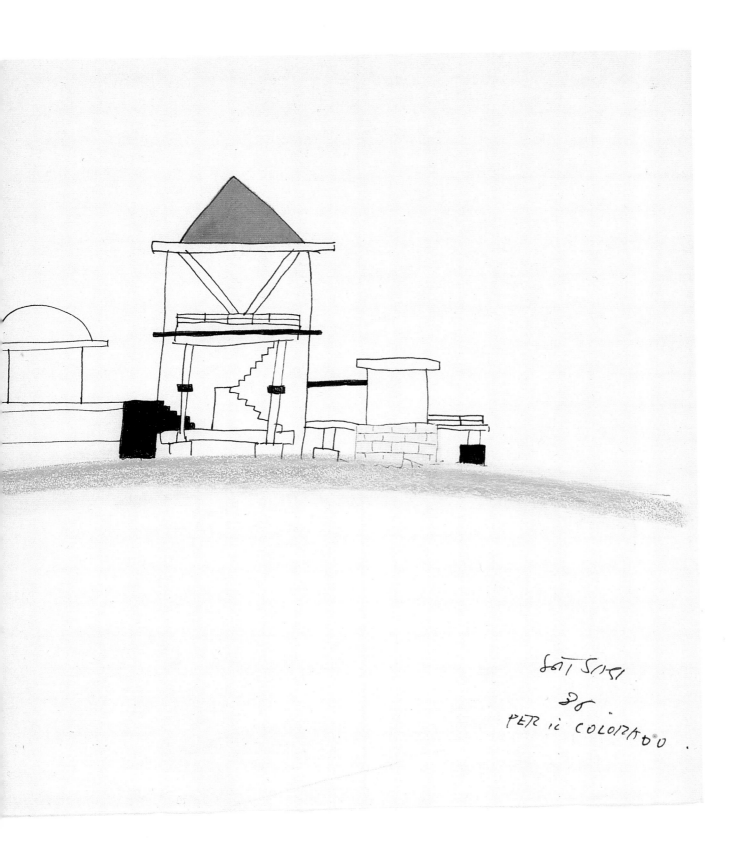

Ǝͻͳ Ͻͳⲅͳ
86
PER il COLORADO .

RIGHT: "Redesign of Seat of Authority," 1978

BELOW: "Proust" armchair, 1978

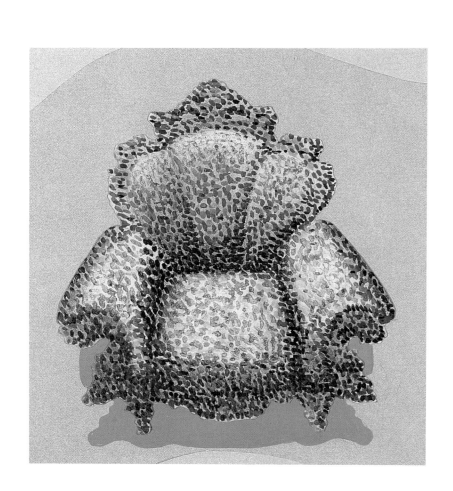

DRAWING FOR TOKYO EXHIBITION CATALOGUE, 1986
Graphite, gouache, and colored pencil on board
H. 39¼ x W. 27½ in. (99.7 x 69.9 cm)
Promised gift of Mathew Wolf

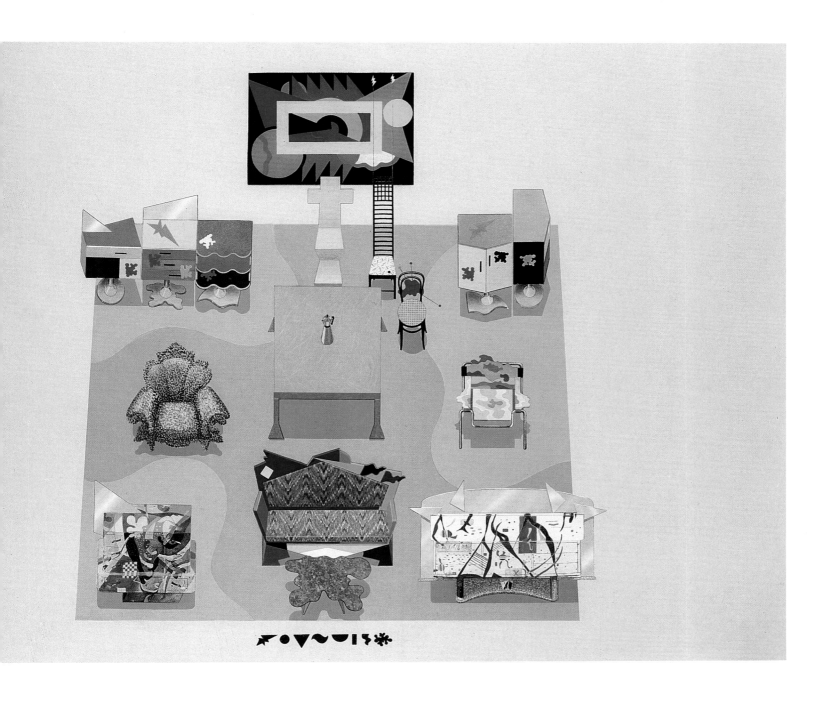

PIERO GILARDI, Italian, born 1942

"I SASSI" (THE ROCKS) SEATING, 1967
Painted polyurethane
Left rock: H. 17¾ x Diam. 23⅝ in. (45.1 x 60 cm)
Manufacturer: Gufram
Purchase, Theodore R. Gamble, Jr., Gift, in honor of
his mother, Mrs. Theodore Robert Gamble, 1987
1987.6.2a–c

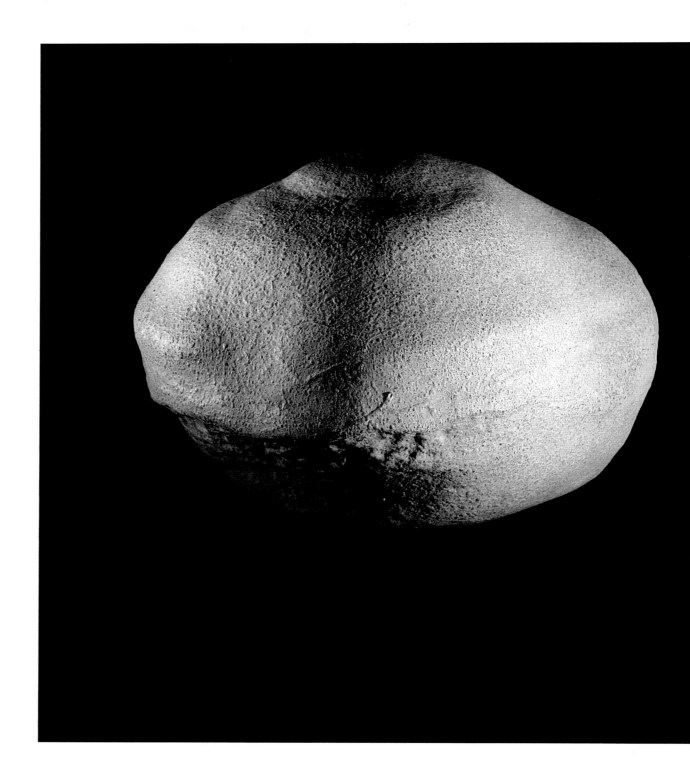

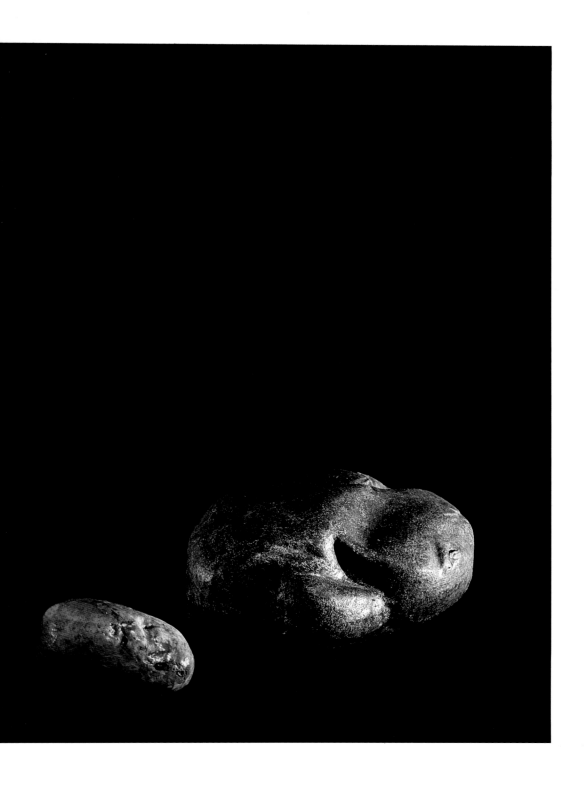

Ettore Sottsass, Jr., Italian, born Austria, 1917

"Tartar" Table, 1985
Reconstituted veneer, lacquer, and plastic laminate
H. 30 x W. 75¾ x D. 32¼ in. (76.2 x 192.4 x 81.9 cm)
Manufacturer: Memphis
Promised gift of Daniel Wolf